THE ECONOMIC CIVILIZATION
OF EUROPE

The Economic Civilization of Europe series provides a new, integrated approach to the related concerns of economists and historians. Blending the techniques of both disciplines, each volume in the series connects political and social developments with the economic circumstances of the period under examination.

HARRY A. MISKIMIN, the author of this volume in The Economic Civilization of Europe series, is Associate Professor of History, Yale University. He is the author of *Money, Prices, and Foreign Exchange in Fourteenth Century France* and numerous articles on the economy of Medieval and Renaissance Europe.

The Economy
of
Early Renaissance
Europe
1300–1460

HARRY A. MISKIMIN

Prentice-Hall, Inc. *Englewood Cliffs, N. J.*

A SPECTRUM BOOK

Current Printing (last number):
10 9 8 7 6 5 4 3 2 1

C–13–234872–1
P–13–234864–0

Library of Congress Catalog Card Number: 69–17375

Printed in the United States of America

Prentice-Hall International, Inc. (*London*)

For
A.S.M., S.A.M., and M.C.M.

Preface

To some, no penance would be sufficient for the sin of attempting to write an economic history of the entirety of Europe, even for a somewhat circumscribed period. To others, however—those perhaps who have felt the need for a synoptic economic history of the era of the Renaissance—it may not seem unreasonable to call upon their charity; first, since the act of compression in itself produces some distortion, not of fact, but of tone; second, since it is inevitable that the selection and exclusion of material and the placing of emphasis are personal decisions and as such bound to diverge from the reader's own special preference. A third demand upon the reader's generosity arises from the obvious and unavoidable dependence upon the work of others which such a project entails. I have included a very limited group of *Suggestions for Further Reading* at the end of this volume, but a complete bibliography is impractical, since it would outweigh the book itself. On the other hand, the bibliographies contained in the books cited should serve to guide the reader to the wider literature of the field.

Finally, I must offer my gratitude to Robert S. Lopez for his care in reading the manuscript with the continuing honesty of a great teacher and the kindness of a friend, and to Alice S. Miskimin for her wifely patience, her wisdom, and her generosity in offering a multitude of suggestions, both stylistic and substantive. The errors are, of course, mine, but they are fewer because of the assistance of these two scholars.

I must also thank the editors of the *Economic History Review* and of the *Journal of Economic History* for permitting me to reprint Graphs I, II, IV, V, and VI, which originally appeared in "The Economic Depression of the Renaissance," *Economic History Review*, XIV, 1962, and Graph VII, which formed part of "Monetary Movements and Market Structures: Forces for Contraction in Fourteenth and Fifteenth Century England," *Journal of Economic History*, XXIV, 1964.

Contents

1
OVERVIEW *1*

2
THE AGRARIAN ECONOMY *14*

TOPOGRAPHY 14

TECHNOLOGY 17

CRISIS AND DEPOPULATION 25

THE LANDLORDS ADJUST 32

England *32*
France *51*
Germany *57*
Scandinavia *59*
Central Europe *60*
Spain *61*
Italy *65*

3
TOWN AND INDUSTRY *73*

POPULATION 73

PROVISIONMENT 77

THE STRUCTURE OF INDUSTRY 81

MARKETS 86

WOOL VERSUS SILK 92

RESTRICTION, REGULATION, AND PESSIMISM 105

MINING 112

4
THE INTERNATIONAL ECONOMY 116

ORIGINS 116

THE TOOLS OF TRADE:
MEDITERRANEAN DOMINANCE 117

THE GOODS EXCHANGED 123

STATISTICS OF TRADE 129

CRISIS 132

DEATH AND DISPLAY 134

THE BALANCE OF PAYMENTS 138
Italians and Hansards 138
The Coffers of Rome 144
Diplomacy 147

THE MEDITERRANEAN SOUTH 150

BEYOND GIBRALTAR 158

5
GOVERNMENT, PROPERTY,
AND THE INDIVIDUAL 164

SUGGESTIONS FOR FURTHER READING 171

INDEX 172

List of Graphs

GRAPH   I   Growth of Town Walls 22

GRAPH   II   Population of England and Catalonia 28

GRAPH   III   Population of Rural Pistoia 31

GRAPH   IV   Population of Nineteen Towns 76

GRAPH   V   Trends in the Cloth Trade: Marseille,
              Florence, Ypres, and England 94

GRAPH   VI   International Trade, 1270–1550 130

GRAPH VII   England, 1273–1470 140

1

Overview

The drama of historical change obscures its antecedents; it is however never unique to the moment of its occurrence, but rather the culmination of a more extended process. When an historian writes of an age of change, an "era of transition," he must refer either to a heightening in the pace of historical development or to an unusual degree of compression and confluence of alterations in the fabric of history. Either of these criteria justify the historian in calling the early years of the fourteenth century an age of change. The forces marshaled by Pope Boniface VIII to defend the Church against the inroads of Edward I of England and Philip IV of France polarized the centuries-old struggle between secular and spiritual authorities and made redefinition of their relative roles imperative. A new and powerful body of secular political thought emerged from the claims and counterclaims of the parties; it was supported and defended by new and more powerful monarchs. The longbow, gunpowder, and improvements in military strategy threatened the nobility with functional obsolescence. The success of the townspeople of Flanders, armed only with pikes, in slaughtering the French knights at Courtrai in 1302 proved that the threat was real. The instability of the agricultural base, the foundation upon which society is built, was revealed only a few years later; the worst famine of the Middle Ages occurred in 1315–17, presenting Europe with the spectre of starvation and the possibility of a general Malthusian food crisis. Before the middle of the century, however, the demographic effects of the famine appeared insignificant in the wake of the Black Death, a Pan-European epidemic of bubonic plague. Each of these forces made an impact upon the economic structure, upon the definition of and justification for property, and upon the economic role of the individual. Each therefore requires consideration for an understanding of the economic history of the fourteenth and fifteenth centuries.

By the middle of the thirteenth century, Scholastic doctrine reached, in the writings of Thomas Aquinas, what Schumpeter has elsewhere called a classical stage. In Thomistic theory, at least, the various segments of society were divinely ordered and placed in harmonious relationship one with the other. Further, the theory, if not the fact, was broadly accepted, and it provided the basic premises within which social conflict could be disputed and resolved. Each individual man, no matter how humble, was possessed of an immortal soul and hence, within the Christian context, each man was valuable in himself. The state was an organ for human fulfillment and for the perfection of society; its end, therefore, was the welfare of the public. The means open to the state in order to attain this end were thus limited to those that were in accord with divine law and the will of God. As long as these conditions were observed, discord would not arise in the relationships between the secular and the sacerdotal authorities. The Church and, hence, the Pope were committed to maintain the spiritual welfare of the people of the earth; the state and the king were equally bound in the secular sphere. Both king and Pope were subject to the laws of God, and since these laws defined both the common end and the respective function of each authority, there was theoretically no need, within the unity imposed by divine sanction, for conflict between them. Within the political realities of this world as well, the two authorities were balanced in counterpoise, with perhaps an edge of power and prestige on the side of the Church in the second half of the thirteenth century. The Pope could excommunicate a recalcitrant monarch and thereby deny him the sacraments. This would jeopardize his access to heaven and, at least as significantly, deny him the loyalty of his subjects, since the excommunication of the king freed them from their oaths of homage and fealty. In more extreme cases, an entire country could be placed under interdict, the churches closed, and solemn marriage, baptism, and burial forbidden. Such weapons were powerful and could, in the thirteenth century, provide a positive check upon the monarchies of Christendom.

In addition to the general limitation upon royal authority implicit in the notion that the state must act on behalf of the public welfare under known rules imposed by God, Aquinas offered a defense of private property. Private ownership was the best form of property division, since it prevented possible disruption of the social order, by providing clearly delineated rules of possession and since it contributed motivation for care in the use of property and for energetic devotion to labor. Human reason, therefore, justified private ownership.

Private property, the inherent value of the individual, and the constraint upon the state to act for the public welfare are economic as well as ethical concepts. If private property is to exist, there is some limitation, however indistinct, upon the governmental right to tax. If the individual is innately valuable, he may neither be enslaved nor treated as a hybrid domestic animal, a beast of burden for the glorification and enrichment of the monarch. If the public good is the object of government, then there is a limit to the self-aggrandizement of the king, and equally, he bears the positive duty to care for the subject. When these political ideas, theoretical though they may be, were sustained by an institution with such power and prestige as the thirteenth-century Catholic Church possessed, they constituted a significant force in the organization, structure, and contemporary conceptions of economic activity and fiscal policy.

A word of caution is necessary: the Thomistic theory of government obviously did not always correspond with practice. The absolutism of Emperor Frederick II (d. 1250) in his Sicilian kingdom is a case in point. He eliminated virtually all local and feudal authority, severely restricted clerical courts, and even went to the extreme of destroying a Genoese fleet carrying Northern bishops to a council called by Pope Gregory IX for the purpose of extending the effects of the sentence of excommunication pronounced against Frederick in 1239. The flavor of Frederick's rule is perhaps best revealed in two rather bizarre experiments attributed by legend to him. In one, it was said, he enclosed a man in a wine cask to prove that the soul died with the body; in the other, to have disemboweled two living men to study the digestive system. Frederick thus showed little evidence of concern for the individual or of the sense of constraint required by papal theory and divine law, but he provides, perhaps, a classic example of the exception that proves the rule. The economic activities of Frederick II, among those of all the rulers of the Middle Ages, are most closely akin to the mercantilist policies of the age of Louis XIV, when the absence of constraint upon the monarchy was one of the chief philosophical tenets of government. If the deviation of Frederick's economic policies from those of contemporary rulers accentuates the importance of philosophical and political premises in economic affairs, the political reality of those premises is demonstrated by the ultimate frustration that Frederick suffered in the face of papal sanction, excommunication, and the concern of other monarchs at his alarming assertion of imperial power.

By the turn of the thirteenth century, however, new forces that were severely to weaken and ultimately to destroy the constraining power of the church were germinating. In 1294, Edward I of England was engaged simultaneously in wars with Scotland and with Wales. A naval incident had resulted in a battle between English and Gascon ships, on the one hand, and Norman ships, on the other. Philip IV of France used this battle as an excuse to confiscate Gascony from Edward. Edward, in his turn, declared war on France and formed an alliance in 1297 with the Count of Flanders. Now the costs of war had risen substantially, and far exceeded the ordinary budgets of either monarch; naval expenses alone in 1295 cost Philip IV more than 1,579,250 *livres tournois,* a sum well in excess of the normal Crown revenues. It was a fiscal and strategic necessity for both monarchs to seek additional revenue, and each logically turned to the greatest source of readily available wealth—the Church.

In the past, the Church had not been unwilling to provide funds for the secular rulers; taxes had been levied on the clergy, with papal consent, to finance the Crusades both in the Holy Land and within Europe itself. Pope Boniface VIII (1294–1303), however, prohibited taxation of the clergy in this instance at precisely the moment when the two strongest monarchies of the West desperately needed funds. Philip IV, by guile, and Edward I, by brute force, continued to obtain the needed funds despite the wishes of the Pope, who denounced the continuing impositions in the bull *Clericis laicos,* decreeing excommunication for any who taxed the clergy and for any who paid the tax. Too much was at stake in the great monarchies to allow this to pass. Edward countered the effect of the bull by denying royal justice to clerics; no cleric could present a complaint in a royal court, but any complaint against a cleric would be heard. This constituted, in effect, the complete removal of royal protection from the Church in England. In France, Philip IV struck back against the bull by prohibiting the export of money from his kingdom and hence the transfer of Church revenues to Rome. Boniface, forced to retreat, was compelled to allow taxation, but he had not yet learned the delicacy of his position. In 1302, he issued the bull *Unam sanctam,* in which he asserted that it was necessary for the "temporal authority to be subject to the spiritual" and that "every human being to be saved must be subject to the Roman pontiff." There is a certain ambiguity about these phrases; if Boniface meant merely that the spiritual was the superior moral guide and, in that sense, higher, the claim was neither unique nor shocking. If, on the other hand, the bull was a direct claim to temporal power, it was the strongest such statement ever issued by the medieval papacy.

Philip IV, with the aid of his Minister, Nogaret, was able to capitalize upon the ambiguity of the bull and to invent and collect sufficient charges and evidence to accuse the Pope of heresy. A request was made for a Church Council to try Boniface, while Nogaret, setting out to arrest him, captured the Pope in his summer palace at Anagni. The latter move ultimately stirred the local population to resist the French and to rescue the Pope from the small band of captors, but it was too late; the shock, and perhaps the abuse, were beyond the recuperative powers of Boniface, then in his mid-eighties. He died shortly thereafter and with him died the medieval phase of the history of the Church. The Church never recovered the prestige it had lost; the transfer of the papacy to Avignon and the election of a French pope in the person of Clement V gave credibility to the charge that the papacy was a tool of the French monarchy during the so-called Babylonian Captivity, 1305–1378. The

Great Schism, which began in 1378 with the simultaneous election of two popes and was not finally resolved until 1417, served only further to reduce the stature of the papacy.

The loss of prestige was accompanied by the birth of a new theory of government, set forth by Marsilius of Padua in the *Defensor Pacis*, 1324. In Marsilius, the dominance of the temporal over the spiritual power is asserted; the state further emerges from the bounds of divine and natural law; it must be obeyed in and for itself. Such doctrine was reinforced in the world of political realities by the royal lawyers' application of imperial Roman law to secular monarchies through the simple formula stating that the king was emperor in his own kingdom. The old stature of the papacy was gone, and new forces had arisen to strengthen the secular state.

These changes, however, had also altered the premises of economic activity. In the absence of a strong papacy counterpoised against the state within the framework of a unified divine law, what force was to assert, even abstractly, the value of the individual? I mean here the ordinary individual and not that exceptional individualist the Renaissance man. Was not part of the defense of private property against the greed of the state vitiated? Finally, the question of the function of the state was henceforth increasingly to become merely a question of the will of the ruler and thus free from the implicit constraint to action on behalf of the public good as defined within the rubric of divine law. Limitations to power remained; the age of absolutism was still in the future, but one of the major steps on the path toward it had been accomplished.

Both in the political and in the economic spheres, the nobility remained a powerful counterbalance to the extension of royal authority. In France at the beginning of the fourteenth century, for example, a number of nobles, both clerical and lay, held the right to issue money—normally a sovereign prerogative. In addition, they could impose certain taxes, restrict or prohibit regional and international movements of goods, and in some cases, levy duties on international trade. In almost all countries, the political power of the nobles gave them the leverage to resist taxation and hence to limit the flow of revenue into the royal coffers. In its turn, this tended to restrict the scope of activities, economic as well as political, that the king could undertake. Many towns, as a result, enjoyed a considerable degree of freedom from royal regulation during the twelfth and thirteenth centuries and many benefited from the struggle between the king and the nobility, receiving royal grants of privilege, charters, or communal status, in return for their support. In the early stages of the reassertion of royal authority, after the breakdown of the ninth and tenth centuries, the granting of freedom from regulation was a more politically feasible method of demonstrating the royal presence than was the attempt to enforce direct control from an inadequate power base. The additional benefit that derived from the creation of an urban force in opposition to the nobility was not ignored by the emerging monarchs.

There were, of course, regional variations across Europe, both in timing and in the extent to which these forces were operative, but in general, the limitations imposed upon the control authority tended to assure considerable latitude for urban economic activity during the twelfth and thirteenth centuries. The centuries-long struggle between Pope and Emperor in Germany, playing as it did upon the animosities between the German nobles and the Emperor in Germany, prevented effective exercise of imperial authority in Italy by diverting the imperial forces to the German hinterland. This allowed the Italian communes to thrive economically and even to involve and to absorb into their economic activities a substantial portion of the local Italian nobility. In Germany also, many towns benefited and were able to establish themselves as relatively independent political units.

England, where the monarchy had retained substantial unity and strength from the time of William the Conqueror, presents a somewhat different instance. Royal charters had been granted to English towns from the end of the eleventh century, and their number increased during the twelfth and thirteenth centuries. Such charters often commuted the various feudal obligations to a single payment and allowed the regulation of economic affairs and various judicial and executive functions to be performed by the local citizens; in addition, the towns were sometimes freed from royal tolls. These privileges were given, however, from a position of relative strength in contrast to similar grants in continental Europe. The barons who forced King John to sign Magna Carta included in it clauses protecting private property and specifying that the King was subject to law, but they did not destroy his power. The monarchy remained unified but under sufficient pressure from the nobles to make any gross violation of the economic interests of the towns politically unwise. On the other hand, the monarchy was strong enough to protect the towns from the nobles, and trade benefited from the presence of a strong, but not overbearing, central authority.

The power and prestige of the nobility in all countries had derived originally from their role as a mounted fighting force; for the nobles to be effective it was necessary for them to possess enough land to sustain themselves and, in the case of the greater nobles, their retainers as well and to provide weapons, armor, and horses for their military enterprises. The land they held for this purpose, either from the king or from lesser landlords who were willing to forego their territorial independence in return for protection, was the basis for their power—power which continued long after the cessation of the services which initially had justified it, power that enabled the nobles to act as a countervailing force with respect to the king. By the beginning of the fourteenth century, however, several factors were acting to undermine the position of the nobility.

The military prowess of the nobles—and hence the validity of their chief justification—had become questionable for a combination of reasons. Subinfeudation, the practice whereby a number of small vassals owed their loyalty to a great vassal rather than directly to the king, had long presented a difficult problem of military discipline and had reduced the value of the feudal army. The geographical and temporal restrictions upon military service—often 40 days within the borders of the country—were equally inconvenient. When possible, therefore, many princes found it efficient to encourage their nobles to substitute money payments for their feudal military obligations, so that the funds received could be used to hire mercenaries whose service was more effective because it was not limited by custom. In England, this practice had been followed by Henry I and Henry II, and although limited by Magna Carta to payments having baronial consent, it remained in use in the fourteenth century. In France, similar commutations of military service to money payments had occurred. For example, in 1304, Philip IV used the right of *arrière-ban*, the royal privilege of calling up every capable man for the defense of the kingdom, as the basis for extracting a substantial tax in lieu of service. Now while the king benefited from the greater military efficiency of mercenaries, the nobility had begun to surrender one of its principal justifications for continuance as an elevated and privileged class. On the other hand, the actual performance of the nobility as a fighting force during the fourteenth century, particularly in France, was appallingly weak, and discretion, a quality relatively rare among the noble class, may truly have been the better part of valor. The century had begun, after all, with the terrible defeat of the French nobles at Courtrai, their charge broken on the pikes of the Flemish artisans. In 1346 at Crécy, in 1356 at Poitiers, and again in 1415 at Agincourt, the English yeoman, armed with the longbow, proved his superiority over the French mounted and heavily armored knight.

That changes in military technology and strategy had undermined the effectiveness of the nobility in carrying out its function as a fighting force was more than evident by the fourteenth century; two consequences emerged. First, since they no longer monopolized military skill, the nobility could be more easily controlled by a government provided with sufficient funds for hiring mercenaries. Second, the same inefficiencies that cost them their unique military position, reduced their value to the prince and hence the strength of their claim to share in the power and support that was increasingly invested in the royal authority. This is not to imply, of course, that the nobility lost all power; power remained in the traditional status of the nobility, in the fact of great wealth and the possession of land, and in their personal compatibility with the king, who remained, in many countries, psychologically and socially a member of the noble class in spite of his wider diplomatic and political interests. In France, after all, it was not until the middle of the seventeenth century that the nobility totally lost its power to lead armed opposition against the king.

As in the military sphere, so too in the economic, new pressures were placed upon the power base of the noble class in the fourteenth and fifteenth centuries. The tendency of landholders to allow the substitution of monetary rent for the labor services due from their peasants had been continuous from the thirteenth century and had left the nobles vulnerable to price inflation that could reduce the real value of their rents. In addition, the commutation of services had given the king, particularly in France, increased leverage over landlords through the weapon of debasement of the coinage; weakening the coinage tended to increase prices, to reduce the intrinsic value of monetary rents, and thus to lower the real income of those who owned land let out for fixed long-term annual payments. Philip IV of France, whom Dante placed in the Inferno as a counterfeiter, was well aware of this weapon and employed it periodically to raise taxes from the great landholders, both secular and lay; it was better to volunteer to pay a contribution or levy than to suffer the effects of debasement. Unfortunately for the landholders, they often ultimately paid on both counts.

Other difficulties also arose to strike at the landholders' incomes. The fourteenth and fifteenth centuries were the period of the Hundred Years' War; nobles who were involved were often absent from their lands, leaving them in the care of self-interested managers who sought their personal profit. Sometimes, too, the nobles went to their deaths, leaving only a minor heir and thus making their estates subject to the costs and potential mismanagement implicit in wardship. In France, the nobility also suffered destruction of crops and of equipment such as mills, ovens, and granaries during the periodic English campaigns of devastation that marked the course of the Hundred Years' War. These factors, in my opinion, however, are of relatively lesser significance when compared to the far-reaching economic consequences of the Black Death, 1348–49. The destruction of a substantial part of the population greatly increased the economic opportunities open to the remaining laborers, and as a result, the price of farm labor rose sharply. The demographic crisis also depressed, or at least held down, the demand for agricultural produce, so that the landholders were caught between rising prices for the factors of production, on the one hand, and falling or stable prices for their output, on the other. The long-run impact of, and response to, these conditions varied from country to country and region to region, but it is safe to say that the initial effect in almost all the countries of western Europe was to weaken the economic power of the nobility. The secondary effects were more complex, as will be shown during the subsequent discussion of agriculture.

The deposition of Richard II of England in 1399, the feud between the Burgundians and the Armagnacs, and the events of the Wars of the Roses provide sufficient evidence to demonstrate that it would be unwise to overemphasize the weakness of the nobility or to overlook the ability, particularly among the greatest landlords, to reconstitute their power. But it would be equally fallacious to underestimate the economic and political crises confronting the nobility in the late fourteenth century. Accompanying the loss of their military monopoly and the diminution of their economic strength there was a very real reduction in the capacity of the noble class to impose limits upon the central figure of monarchy, the king. In fact, far from opposing royal authority, the nobility were forced by circumstance to appeal directly to the king for aid in their economic distress and to seek maximum wage laws and other restrictive legislation deemed necessary to prevent peasants from abandoning the fields in order to raise their income, either elsewhere in agriculture or in the towns. Such appeals constituted, in effect, an open invitation by the nobility for the extension of royal authority on so national a scale that royal power henceforth would touch the lives of the great majority of the population. It arose as the immediate consequence of the economic weakness of the landholding class and provided new precedents for government intervention in economic affairs. In France, this occurred to so great an extent that it is not really stretching a point to seek in this period and in the economic policies of such kings as Charles VII (1422–61) and Louis XI (1461–83) the origins of the policy of governmental interference and control that subsequently grew into mercantilism.

In fact, precisely the same crises which weakened and eroded the economic and military power base of the noble class, reducing their capacity to resist the increasing imposition of royal authority, simultaneously compelled the monarchies to intervene more directly throughout the entire economy. The Black Death of 1348–49 and the subsequent visitations of bubonic plague disrupted the urban economy, created population vacuums, and led to massive internal migrations. Royal governments, as a result, were drawn into the field of guild and town legislation and were forced, as well, to formulate strictly defensive measures in agriculture. The new military technology impelled governments to search for new sources of funds and new and more broadly based taxes; the increased control of the guilds and the towns provided one ready-to-hand source for such funds, one that became increasingly significant as the fifteenth century progressed. The prolonged duration and the increased geographical extent of the wars of the fourteenth and fifteenth centuries necessitated large exports of specie in diplomatic and military expenditures. This trend was reinforced by an enhanced desire for luxury consumption, stimulated, perhaps, by the imminence of death during the series of spectacular plagues that swept Europe in the second half of the fourteenth century. As a result, balance of payments problems, for many countries, became questions of military as well as economic necessity, and again the royal governments were forced to seek remedies—remedies that inevitably drew the monarchies further into the management and control of economic affairs. In the reign of Edward III, for example, control of the English wool staple, in addition to serving as a source of funds for the king, became a direct adjunct to his French war policy: Edward used it as a lever to force the wool-hungry cloth towns of Flanders into an alliance with England. Philip VI used his control of the grain supplies of northern France as a counterweapon in an endeavor to starve the Flemish into submission and swing them to the side of the French. Economic policy had become a major weapon in the arsenal of state power.

Of necessity, the role of the royal governments in economic affairs grew to serve the new needs of the state during a period of crisis and institutional change. The events which weakened the nobility at once allowed and required the extension of royal power over an ever broadening segment of the economy. Many of these same events, conjoined with other more specific factors to weaken the Church, since its power was also partially derived from the ownership of land. But the more serious loss was that dramatized by the capture and imprisonment of the Pope at Anagni—the decline of the international spiritual stature of the Church. The two most substantial political forces of the thirteenth century—the nobility and the papacy—had suffered serious defeats by the late fourteenth century. Consequently, the constraints of divine law had become somewhat more remote from the day-to-day business of monarchies, and the public good more closely identified with the pleasure of the king. Henceforward, the line of authority from the king to the individual would be more direct, less mitigated by the forces of the Church or the nobility. The importance of the actions of the central government upon both the conceptualization and the actual conduct of economic affairs grew in direct proportion to the degree that *princeps legibus solutus est*—a formula of the ancients, but one incorporated into a French ordinance of August, 1374.

2

The Agrarian Economy

TOPOGRAPHY

Dramatic and imposing as the actions of princes, popes, and nobles may be, and as significant as the interactions among them are for economic behavior and accomplishment in the later Middle Ages, one must not forget that the greatest portion of the population, perhaps nine-tenths, were agricultural workers. Agriculture was by far the predominant economic activity during this period, and it remained so until well into the nineteenth century. It was upon an agricultural base that medieval society was constructed, and it was the peasant, through his humble labors, who created the conditions that made possible the intellectual and cultural triumphs of the Middle Ages. The importance of agriculture is self-evident. How, then, was it conducted? What conditions determined its success and its organization? In order to seek answers, we must begin with certain elementary facts regarding the physical configurations of the European continent.

A glance at a contour map of Europe reveals two distinct relief patterns that run in an east–west direction and divide the continent into two regions along a line placed roughly between 45 and 50 degrees latitude. Most of Spain, southeastern France, Switzerland, most of Italy with the exception of the Po Valley, Greece, the Balkan Peninsula below the Carpathian mountains but excluding the Danube Basin, and much of Asia Minor comprise mountainous regions with elevations generally greater than fifteen hundred feet above sea level. To the north, starting with southern

14

England and the western coast of France and then continuing in a wedge widening to include the coast of Sweden, a great plain extends to the Urals in the east and to the Caucasus in the south. In this flat region, the elevation rarely exceeds 600 feet above sea level.

Throughout both regions, which together encompass the Iberian Peninsula, France, the Low Countries, Sweden, Denmark, England, Germany, and much of central Europe, the average rainfall is between 20 and 40 inches annually. This uniformity is more apparent than real, however. For rainfall to be useful to agriculture, it must be properly distributed over the course of the year; thus one extremely wet month in a year, while it may yield 30 or 40 inches of rain, does not necessarily provide the basis for a prosperous agricultural civilization. Attention to a few of the many factors that affect the patterns of rainfall and climate is necessary for even a broad outline of the role of such patterns in the cultivation of the land.

The prevailing wind in western Europe blows from the southwest, carrying air, tempered by the softening influence of the Atlantic, far into the vast European plain and contributing to the relatively mild climate of this region. From the Russian plains, on the contrary, a high pressure front of cold air typically extends along the mountainous border formed by the Pyrenees, the Alps, and the Caucasus. This front, in conjunction with the far northern Arctic air mass, forms a corridor bounding the warmer Atlantic air on both the north and the south. Within this corridor, tracing the great European plain, rainfall is evenly distributed, summers are wet, and the temperature is moderate. The June-to-September rainfall, for example, averages nine inches in London and almost ten inches in Berlin; this may be contrasted to five inches in Rome or a mere two and one-half inches in Lisbon during the same summer months.

The southern elevated regions of Europe generally are cut off by Spain from the climatological influences of the Atlantic and consequently they display rainfall patterns quite distinct from those of the northern plains. Rainfall tends to be concentrated in the fall or early winter, when the land-based air cools and contrasts with the air influenced by the still warm Mediterranean Sea. April again witnesses increased rainfall in Italy and along the Dalmatian coast when the coastal air warms before the snow melts on the cooler mountain reaches, producing a contrast in temperature favorable to precipitation; as the spring progresses, the temperature differential diminishes, and the summers are dry. Summer drought is also a problem in the Iberian Peninsula, although the average rainfall varies greatly across Spain, dropping from about 66 inches annually in the northwest to a mere 10 inches in the southeast.

Soil belts roughly corresponding to the rainfall belts traverse Europe. In the Mediterranean lands, the soil is light and tends to be dry; since the climate is warm, the evaporation of ground water exceeds the rainfall, so that the mineral content of the soil is not depleted by leaching. On the steeper slopes, however, the converse process predominates because of the rapid runoff. To the north, in the great lowland plain of Europe, lie the so-called humid brown earths—heavy, deeply wetted soils, but sufficiently rich in residual, glacial mineral content to be fertile and sufficiently flat to avoid excessive leaching. These soils, however, do require the addition of organic fertilizer and humus to sustain intensive cultivation. To the east, of course, is the black-earth district of Russia, where cold winters and rapid summer evaporation prevent the destruction of humus derived from the grass plains. This soil is naturally fertile and demands less artificial fertilizer than do the soils of the plains of western Europe.

One further feature of European topography, forestation, remains to be discussed. The exceptions to any general rule are even greater here than elsewhere, but it is possible to identify three broad forest groups. To the north, in Scandinavia, Russia, and northern Scotland, is the coniferous forest zone that yielded the fir and pine used for the masts and spars of ships and also provided pitch and other naval stores. In the central region, including a portion of Portugal, northwest Spain, England, France, and Germany, deciduous forests of beech and oak predominate. Along the Mediterranean coast, the forests are essentially scrub growth and olive, varied along the upward slopes of the mountainous regions by oak and then pine. The region at the head of the Adriatic benefited from the diversity of conditions along the Po Valley and the base of the Alps to produce a considerable growth and variety of trees. Similar conditions prevailed along the edges of the Black Sea.

Enough has been said to provide, at least in outline, some conception of the general topography of Europe. It is here that any discussion of agriculture should begin, since these are the basic factors that determine the nature and define the problems of regional agriculture in Europe. A cautionary word is required, however: regional disparities in climate have been argued by scholars of renown and otherwise as causal determinants of differences in artistic talent, intelligence, ambition, skin color, and even in the nature of government necessary to a particular region. Generalization of this sort is more than moderately suspect; even in reference to such a seemingly direct connection as appears to exist between the soil and the crop sustained thereon, many special cases and exceptions prevent the too facile formulation of broad theories.

TECHNOLOGY

Perhaps the single most profound advance in agricultural technology during the Middle Ages was the replacement of the two-field system by the three-field system of crop rotation. In the former, one-half the arable land was allowed to lie fallow each year, with the obvious result that in any given harvest year, vast acres of farm land contributed nothing. Under the three-field system, which began to spread across Europe from about the end of the eighth century, only one-third of the land was fallow at a time. The first field was planted in the fall with rye or winter wheat and was harvested in the early summer; the second field was planted in the spring with oats, beans, or peas and was harvested in the late summer; the third field remained fallow. In each subsequent year, the fields changed places in the rotation, so that the fallow field of one year became the winter wheat field of the next, and so forth, until each field had been utilized once in each manner over a three-year period.

The potential increase in output which could result from a switch from the two- to the three-field system has been clearly set forth by Lynn White in his *Medieval Technology and Social*

Change.[1] In the example he presents, he maintains that since the fallow was plowed twice a year from the twelfth century onward, a two-field cultivation of a 600-acre farm would require 900 acres of plowing for 300 acres of crops. On a three-field system, the same farm with only 200 acres of fallow would require only 800 acres of plowing for 400 acres in crops. Further, since the workers who did the hundred acres of extra plowing under the two-field system would be freed under the three-field system, 75 additional acres of land could be cultivated, the 25 fallow acres being plowed twice. Observe that if such new land was available, the productive acreage could increase from 300 to 450, a rise of 50 per cent; if output corresponded directly with the new acreage under cultivation, the increase would surely have been dramatic.

Now, one of the most difficult problems in the history of technology lies in moving from the first evidence of the introduction of a new technique to the methods and degree of its diffusion. While the three-field system had advantages so obvious that one would be led to expect its immediate and universal adoption, this was never the case. By the fourteenth century, 600 years after the first solid evidence of the three-field system, its use was far from universal; even in the recorded instances of its employment, there often is indication that only a small portion of the lands of the recording estate were operated under this system. Many factors delayed application of the three-field rotation. In some regions, its use was rendered impossible or difficult by the climate; as we have seen above, the rainfall in the coastal regions of the Mediterranean was scant in the late spring and summer, the period in which it was most vital for a spring-sown rotation. For this reason the two-course rotation predominated in the southern lands, and the agricultural techniques of classical times remained virtually unaltered. In the far north, on the contrary, the cold winters limited the growth of winter wheat and dictated a two-course rotation based upon spring-sown crops.

The plains region, then, was the domain of the three-course rotation; England, France north of the Loire, Germany, and a portion of the Netherlands had the climatic conditions appropriate

[1] Lynn White, Jr., *Medieval Technology and Social Change* (Oxford: Clarendon Press, 1962), pp. 71, 72.

for exploitation of the method, but even in this relatively ideal portion of Europe, there were many exceptions. One of the difficulties was institutional; the switch from a two- to a three-course rotation required redistribution of the land among the tenants. Each farmer had to hold land in all three fields; otherwise his food supply would suffer serious dislocations over the course of the three-year cycle. The medieval surplus was always small, and therefore an excessive portion of land in fallow would, in all probability, literally have meant starvation for the afflicted tenant. As a result, the impediments to the introduction of the three-field system included custom, traditional tenure, and simply the absence of a consensus in favor of the switch.

On newly cleared lands, on reclaimed marshes, or in areas of new colonization, traditional land divisions did not hamper the use of the triennial rotation, and consequently it could be more readily applied in these regions. Perhaps the evidence, limited at best, that the spring crops constituted only a fraction of the total crops—that is, that the three-course rotation was utilized only on a small portion of some estates—may be interpreted as an indication that the system was introduced primarily on assarts, or newly cleared land, while on older segments, subject to traditional tenure arrangements, the institutional obstacles were so great as to prevent more general extension of the system.

Happily, however, new land was available for colonization during the twelfth and thirteenth centuries. The many new villages of France that were founded in the twelfth century and the wave of German colonization that marched eastward from this period until the late thirteenth century attest to the extension of agriculture and to the possibility of employing the improved techniques on new lands unrestricted by custom. For both reasons—the expansion of arable land and the gain in productivity resultant upon the three-field system—the food supplies of Europe grew. Concomitant with the increase in the supply of food, there was a great increase in the population, at once sustained by and contributing to the advance in agricultural production. The best available statistics of population, compiled by J. C. Russell, relate to England; they show growth from the time of the Domesday survey in 1086, when the population was about 1,100,000, until a figure of 3,750,000 was reached in the middle of the fourteenth century.[2] Present statistics for Europe as a whole are perhaps little more than enlightened guesswork blessed, however, by a certain broad consistency among their creators. In general, these estimates indicate at least a doubling of the population of Europe during the three centuries between 1000 and 1300.

The demographic expansion provided workers as well as consumers for the products of the soil; urban concentration increased, and more specialized markets for food were developed as more men devoted themselves solely to urban occupations. The advantages of interregional trade and economic specialization in all probability generated additional gains in productivity as a result of the economic law of comparative advantage. The three-field system fostered the growth of both specialization and productivity, since it provided a surplus for the provisioning of the towns and also because it allowed the support of more horses through the greater supply of fodder crops such as oats in the spring sowing. The use of horses in farming was, for many reasons, an advance; one of the principal advantages, of course, was greater speed than the traditional slow-moving ox provided. With the horse, the region of cultivation around a village or town could be extended outward, so that larger cultivated areas could be used for the sustenance of more concentrated population centers. Perhaps equally significant, less time was lost in moving men, goods, and equipment from one area to another, and the reduction of transit time meant further improvement in agricultural productivity. Additional laborsaving occurred through the reduction in the number of persons required for the operation of a plow; a horse plow needed only one man, whereas a team of oxen was usually worked by three. Similar advantages were derived from the development and employment, in the thirteenth century, of a four-wheeled wagon with a pivoted front axle. The older, two-wheeled cart could be replaced once the solution to the technological problem of maneuvering the four-wheeled version had been found. Having the more advanced wagon meant that greater quantities of food could be transported for longer distances at less cost, and thus it further contributed to the

[2] J. C. Russell, *British Medieval Population* (Albuquerque: University of New Mexico Press, 1948), p. 280. See Graph II, p. 28.

growth of urban market centers, as the centers themselves contributed to the diffusion and employment of the new wagons.

One indication of the growth of the urban as well as of the general population is the growth of town walls shown in Graph I.

It is apparent from the graph that substantial urbanization occurred in the northern region during the years after 1100 and, further, that the rate of growth was maintained over several centuries, finally coming to a peak in the period 1200 to 1250. It must be granted, however, that the expansion of existing walls affords only a rough measurement of population growth that is difficult to interpret in the absence of evidence regarding population density; after the last wall has been built, population may continue to grow, and perhaps a wall may be erected in anticipation of growth that is never realized. Equally plausible, particularly during the Hundred Years' War (1337–1453), is the possibility that a new wall may have been built to replace an existing, damaged wall, but traversing the shortest distance between two outcropping sections of the old wall. This would appear as an extension, although it would in no way be related to demographic variations. Despite such reservations, the graph broadly reflects an increase in the population concentrated in urban centers and nourished by exploitation of the increasingly wide geographical areas from which towns were compelled to seek their foodstuffs.

The figures reflecting the development of the Italian towns are included here for several reasons. They illustrate the chronological precedence of Italian urbanization over its northern counterpart; the Italian peak occurs in the period 1150 to 1200, approximately 50 years in advance of the northern maximum. More importantly, however, the southern figures are meant to serve as a caution against too directly correlating new agricultural techniques and increased urbanization. As the previous discussion has shown, southern agriculture was not in general the beneficiary of technological advances comparable to those of the north; the three-field system never took hold, and agriculture remained more or less at the same level it had reached in ancient times. New land was cleared, marshes were drained from an early date, and, particularly in the Po Valley, dikes and embankments were built, but the sum of this activity was of far less significance than the vast efforts of clearing and coloniza-

GRAPH I
Growth of Town Walls

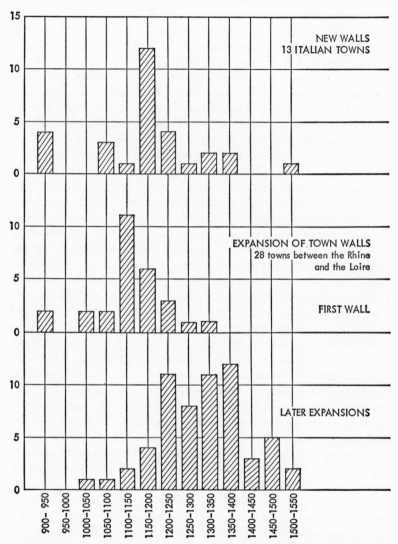

Sources: J. C. Russell, "Late Ancient and Medieval Population," *Trans. of the Amer. Philos. Soc.,* Vol. 48, Part 3, 1958; *Enciclopedia Italiana,* articles on Genoa, Pisa, Florence, Milan, Parma, Pavia, and Lucca; F. L. Ganshof, *Etude sur le développement des villes entre Loire et Rhin au Moyen Age,* Presses Universitaires de France, Paris, 1943.

tion that had been undertaken in northern Europe. The agricultural hinterlands of such great Italian cities as Genoa, Florence, and Venice were never adequate to feed their populations, and hence agricultural revolution cannot be viewed as a causative factor in their early and impressive growth. The case is rather the reverse; as the cities grew, more pressure was put on the food supply; all available land was rapidly brought into production, but this was still insufficient. The hungry communes then, as their counterparts to the north, sought to extend their sources of supply, but with one great distinction. Territorial extension was restricted within the geographical limits set by the mountains and the sea, while technological improvement was retarded by the climate. The cities could increase their agricultural supply only through international trade. Florence, for example, imported nearly two-thirds of her grain supply from lands beyond her territorial jurisdiction during the fourteenth century. Venice, Florence, and other large cities sought their supplies in Apulia, Sicily, the Maremma (the coastal regions of Tuscany), the Balkan Peninsula, and even the Black Sea ports and the Byzantine East. The Italian cities solved the problem of food supply by seeking an ever expanding and distant range of agricultural resources.

The great triumphs of the medieval cities in finding adequate quantities of food entailed certain dangers. It is a commonplace of military strategy that the greater the distance the supply lines must stretch, the more tenuous is the position; this was equally true of the medieval towns. The more efficiently and broadly the towns exploited the surrounding and distant regions, the more danger there was that a slight crisis, political or agricultural, would disturb the balance of the food supply. A city which had sought its food in every corner that reasonably could be reached by ship or wagon had made itself vulnerable to famine, since, as Malthus later observed, the population tended, under normal conditions, to increase in proportion to the food supply. When famine came, the very efficiency of the normal food-gathering process became a curse, since the outer limits of transportation and production had become the normal limits of supply.

In terms of the quality of land as well as of its distance from consumption centers, the agrarian economy of Europe was beginning, by the early fourteenth century, to show signs of having over-reached itself. The new land pressed into service to sustain and support the growing population often was land that initially had been passed by when the demand for agricultural products was smaller. Such land required more intensive cultivation and fertilization in order to maintain even the minimal medieval yields. The figures for yields are usually expressed in terms of the ratio of the seed sown to the havest. While there are numerous statistical problems in measuring these ratios, it appears that a farmer could expect to harvest about four, and sometimes five, bushels of wheat for every bushel sown. The yields for barley were roughly comparable, for rye somewhat higher at six or seven bushels per bushel sown, and for oats rather less at two and one-half to three bushels per bushels sown. Measured in bushels per acre, the yields for wheat seem to have been somewhere between eight and ten bushels, but the reserve for seed must be subtracted, thus dropping the yield to between six and eight bushels an acre. If one-half the fallow land under the three-field system is imputed to wheat production, the net yield is further reduced to between four bushels and five and one-third bushels per acre.

Now, at such low returns, measured either by the seed/yield ratio or by the number of bushels per acre, a very slight decline will make a great percentage difference, and unfortunately for the men of the later Middle Ages, certain factors did exist that tended to create such a decline. Marginal lands which were cleared and farmed as a result of population pressure might produce a reasonable harvest for a number of years, but inevitably their productivity tended to fail. Evidence of soil erosion on presently worthless land that was cultivated in the thirteenth century provides grim documentation of one of the costs of excessive clearing and over-exploitation. In the same context, the three-field system, by medieval standards, was an intensive cultivation and, when practiced on the soils of the lowland plain of Europe, such agriculture required the addition of substantial quantities of fertilizer if it was to be successful for any sustained period. The chief source of fertilizer was, of course, grazing herds of animals; the quantity of animals was to a large extent a function of the amount of available pasture. But under the three-field system, the amount of fallow available for pasture was reduced to one-third, and further, as land was cleared and converted to arable, natural pasture land was reduced. The requirement for manure was increased by the very agricultural expansion that reduced its supply. Under such circumstances, it is not surprising that there is some evidence of falling yields. On the English manor of Wistow, for example, the seed/yield ratio appears to have fallen from about six bushels per bushel sown, in the middle of the thirteenth century, to about three bushels per bushel sown, in the second quarter of the fourteenth century. Less dramatic, but still significant, the fall on the estates of the Bishop of Winchester carried the ratio from 4.3 in the period 1200–1249 to 3.8 in the period 1250–1349. During the same period, the population of England had only slightly less than doubled.

The evidence of falling yields is neither clear nor universal, but Postan and Titow have well illustrated the precariousness of the balance between the food supply and the population in England.[3] Their figures for the middle of the thirteenth century and onward show a very close correlation between grain prices and the payment of heriots, a fee due at the death of a tenant and usually paid in livestock, although money was sometimes employed. Each increase in the price of grain corresponded to a decrease in the population, presumably through malnutrition. There is increasing indication that Europe, by the beginning of the fourteenth century, was pressing against the technological upper limit of its food supplies.

CRISIS AND DEPOPULATION

In the years 1315–17, this fact became devastatingly apparent. During the year 1314, abnormally great rainfall had adversely affected crops, and prices had begun to rise over Europe generally. In 1315, the weather became worse; a true famine developed, striking all the countries of Europe from the Atlantic to Russia, although some of the Mediterranean countries seem to have fared better. By 1316, virtually all of the surplus stores of grain had been consumed. Between May, 1314, and November, 1315, the price of wheat in

[3] M. Postan and J. Titow, "Heriots and Prices on Winchester Manors," *Economic History Review*, 2nd Ser., XI, 1959.

Paris increased fivefold, from .322 to 1.613 livres/hectolitre; in England from July, 1314, to April, 1316, the wheat price at Cuxham rose from 8 to 23 shillings per quarter. In the great Flemish cloth towns of Ypres, Ghent, and Bruges, which like their Italian counterparts had far out grown their local food supplies, the suffering was intense; from May to October, 1316, 2,794 persons died in the town of Ypres alone—probably the equivalent of 10 per cent of the population. The hunger was so deep that instances of cannibalism were reported in some chronicles. By the fall of 1316, the crisis had passed in most European countries, although it continued in Germany for a few months of the following year.

The famine of 1315–17 was one of the most spectacular in the fourteenth and fifteenth centuries, but it was not an isolated phenomenon; it was rather the worst among many smaller and regional famines with similar, if lesser, consequences. There is no general history of famines, but one scholar, Helen Robbins, has compared famine years in France and England over the course of the fourteenth century.[4] For France, she lists the years 1304, 1305, 1310, 1315, 1330–34, 1344, 1349–51, 1358–60, 1371, 1374–75, and 1390; at least on a local basis, in the Paris region, it is necessary to add 1322 and 1325 to the list. For England, she finds famine in 1315–16, semi-famine in 1321, and famine in 1351 and 1369. In portions of southern France, the years 1312, 1313, 1323, 1329, 1335–36, 1337, 1343, and 1361 witnessed local famines in addition to the more general famines considered above. The list of famines could be expanded to include other countries, to comprehend more local and regional occurrences, and to take into account conditions of scarcity that, although falling short of general starvation, still took a certain toll of the population. For France particularly, one might include the periods of English invasion, when agriculture was disrupted and the fields burned. Even without such an expansion to incorporate political disasters, the list of food crises is long enough to suggest that the balance between food production and population had been upset by the beginning of the fourteenth century, if not somewhat earlier. By 1300, almost every child born in western Eu-

[4] Helen Robbins, "A Comparison of the Effects of the Black Death on the Economic Organization of France and England," *Journal of Political Economy*, XXXVI (1928), 447–79.

rope faced the probability of extreme hunger at least once or twice during his expected 30 to 35 years of life.

The consequences of frequent and widespread hunger are more complex than the initial discomfort or death. An extended period of substandard diet may weaken the population as a whole, rendering it more vulnerable to contagious disease; it may, perhaps, physiologically affect the birthrate, although present evidence on this point is unclear. It will certainly affect infant mortality, and hence have considerable impact upon the age structure of the population and consequently upon the over-all productivity of the society. In the later Middle Ages, one direct effect of hunger was an increase in geographical mobility. When the ordinary food supplies failed, the only chance of survival frequently was migration, either to another region or to some center of distribution or charity where larger stores of food were maintained. Monasteries, convents, and cities provided such meager bread distributions as existed, and thus it was not uncommon during periods of famine for masses of people to descend upon the local population centers, the cities, and the larger towns, in search of food. Obviously such emigration would further dissipate the urban supplies and also perhaps lower the potential for recovery by removing some of the productive workers from the land at precisely the moment when their efforts were most needed.

In addition, internal migration in search of food tended to break down the relative isolation of the smaller village and agricultural communities and hence, by reducing the effectiveness of the natural quarantine imposed by village life in the Middle Ages, contributed to the spread of contagious disease among a population already somewhat weakened by hunger. It is not uncommon, even in some sections of the modern world, for pestilence to follow in the wake of famine; the fourteenth century was indeed an age of pestilence. Epidemics had existed in medieval Europe before the fourteenth century, but it was in this period that their frequency and severity were vastly increased and that their impact became virtually universal.

In 1348, after making its European debut at the Crimean port of Caffa, on the Black Sea, the bubonic plague, or Black Death, spread across Europe, passing from Italy through Spain and south-

ern France and then sweeping over almost all of northern Europe
by 1350. Virtually all contemporary records speak of the terror and
of the overwhelming presence of death; the very frequent changes
in the handwriting of the surviving documents suggest that the
chroniclers themselves were often among the victims. It is under-
standable, therefore, that the chroniclers succumbed to their tendency to exaggerate quantities and that they occasionally recorded
a total number of fatalities greater than the entire population of
the recording town. The chronicles remain, however, a valuable
expression of the psychological impact of the plague upon contemporary witnesses. Graph II presents some of the available statistical evidence.

GRAPH II

Population of England and Catalonia
(Expressed as a Percentage of the Maximum)

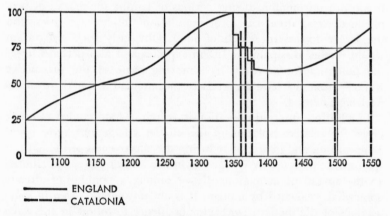

━━━━━━ ENGLAND
━ ━ ━ ━ CATALONIA

SOURCES: J. C. Russell, *British Medieval Population*, University of New Mexico Press, Albuquerque, 1948, Fig. 10.4, p. 280; J. Vicens Vives, *Historia económica de España*, Editorial Teide, Barcelona, 1959.

The graph is cast in percentage terms so as to facilitate international comparison and to reveal the relative rates of growth and
decline more readily than would be the case with absolute figures.
The steep and sudden drop in the English population in 1350 is,
of course, the result of the Black Death, but equally significant

declines occurred fairly regularly at ten-year intervals thereafter. It is a tenet of demography that a great crisis is normally followed by a sharp rise in the birthrate, in compensation for the loss of population during the initial crisis. In this case, however, the rapid succession of country-wide plagues in England during the third quarter of the fourteenth century, in conjunction with the periodic outcroppings of local and regional epidemics that continued until well into the fifteenth century, in effect canceled whatever recuperative powers remained in the population after the initial plague. Indeed, more than 200 years appear to have been required for the reconstitution of the English population. The figures for Catalonia, along with other available statistical materials, suggest that the continental experience was not dissimilar to that of England.

If overpopulation was haunting Europe at the beginning of the fourteenth century, the situation was totally reversed by the end of that century; where five men had been before, three remained—in a world very much altered and seen, perhaps, through different eyes. Whereas land had been scarce before the series of plagues, labor now had become the key factor in agricultural production. In many places, land had become in the absence of labor to till it, worthless; in others, its value was vastly reduced. Further, since the loss of population was at least as great in the crowded and densely inhabited towns and cities as it was in the more wholesome environment of the countryside, the demand for basic goods declined sharply. With falling demand came a relative decrease in the price of grain as compared to prices of luxury foodstuffs and manufactured goods, which rose sharply. By creating a scarcity of labor without initially affecting the quantity of available land, depopulation increased the marginal productivity of the surviving workers, and also, since the price of grain remained quite stable despite its weakening relative position, what an economist would call the marginal revenue product of labor, the price of the output times the amount produced by the last unit of labor added, almost certainly rose. With it, as those imbued with classical economics will have anticipated, rose the price of labor. In England, taking the years 1261–1350 as a base period equal to 100, a composite average of the unadjusted money prices of wheat, rye, barley, and peas declined to a figure of 99 in the 50-year span 1351–1400; during the same period, the price for labor in threshing rose to 133, while the cost of employing reapers increased to 151. The sharp increase in the price of labor, of course, reflected the increased productivity enjoyed by farm workers in a situation of land superfluity.

An excess of land relative to labor implies, of course, a decline in the marginal productivity of the land and thus, given the stability of grain prices, a decreasing marginal revenue product of land and consequently, falling earnings or rents. This theoretical proposition is amply justified by statistics available from widely dispersed geographical areas. In Pistoia, for example, the rent of land paid in wheat declined 40 per cent on average, in the years 1351–1425, from its level in the preceding 75-year span; in France, at the Abbey of St. Germain-des-Prés, money rents dropped 34 per cent, in the period 1422–61, from the average for 1360–1400; in Norfolk, England, the drop was 30.4 per cent from 1376–78 to 1422–60. Rents naturally reflect the real economic return of the land, and if one moves from statistics and economic theory to the mundane level of common sense, the factors at work are equally apparent. The landholder who chose to work his own land was faced with a falling price for his output and with sharply increased costs of production in the form of labor and the minimal amount of machinery required by medieval agricultural technology. Worse still, however, even if he were willing and able to pay the price, it was not certain that he could find labor available when it was required. Legislation promulgated in many countries and designed to reduce the "excessive" demands of wage earners tended, in fact, to create a kind of black market for labor, in which, since the legal wage rate was below the economic wage rate, the landlord was compelled to violate the law if he hoped to prevent labor from seeking alternative employment.

Statistics specifically concerned with the rural population are rare indeed, but qualitative evidence abounds to support the thesis that there was a general migration from the land by peasants and farm laborers. Restrictive legislation enacted to prevent this phenomenon testified to its reality, while the successive passage of such acts confirms their failure to control the flow of workers from the land. Laborers continued to seek their own best interests and they often found, for reasons that will appear later on, that it lay in the

towns. In many cases, consequently, the towns appear to have recovered from the plague more rapidly than the countryside—a development that can be explained only by migration. For one Italian
region, that of Pistoia, rural statistics do exist; they are presented
in Graph III.

GRAPH III
Population of Rural Pistoia

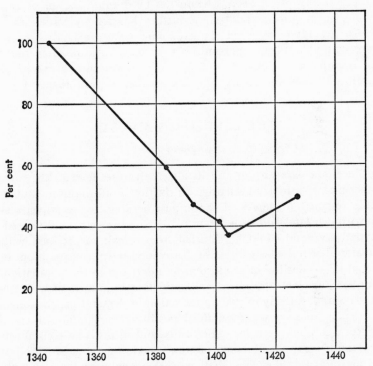

SOURCE: D. Herlihy, "Population, Plague, and Social Change in Rural Pistoia,"
Economic History Review, XVIII, 1965.

As is apparent from Graph III, rural depopulation amounted,
by 1404, to more than 60 per cent of the pre-plague population—
a decline considerably in excess of that recorded in the town of
Pistoia itself and far greater than that present in the over-all figures,
cited above, for either England or Catalonia. In view of the sharp

deviation of the Pistoiese statistics from those series that reflect urban as well as rural experience, it seems possible to explain the steep and continuous decline in the population of the Pistoiese countryside only in terms of migration from the land. Workers were abandoning the fields to better themselves in the towns.

Let us recapitulate the position of the landlord. He was struggling against rising labor costs and the inadequacy of the labor supply at any price; he was hampered by diminishing, or at best stable, grain prices; and he was further harmed by falling rent, which accurately reflected the economic value of land, now in excess supply. What opportunities were open to him? How could he recoup, or at least defend, his former pre-eminent position? Logic and economic theory suggest a number of possibilities.

THE LANDLORDS ADJUST

England

Since land was surplus and its alternative uses few, a shift from labor-intensive to land-intensive cultivation would appear a plausible response to depressed conditions; herding, for example, employs much land and little labor as compared to cereal culture. Alternatively, land could be diverted from cereals to products with greater demand elasticity than basic foodstuffs; consumption of bread might decline in proportion to a decrease in the population, but beer, wine, meats, butter, and agricultural products such as dyestuffs were less likely to share a reduction in demand proportionate to demographic crises. As a third possibility, a landholder could accept a minimal rent for some of his land in order to concentrate his limited supply of labor on the remaining land. A corollary proposition would suggest that by working only the best land, the labor cost per bushel of product would be reduced. For example, labor and capital formerly employed in mending dikes, maintaining drainage or irrigation systems, and coaxing slim yields from reluctant and sterile soils would be conserved by abandoning such lands, and this portion of the average cost per unit of output would fall as the average productivity of the remaining land rose. A fourth path was open to the landowner if he could artificially depress the

wage rate: legislation backed by force, for example, might compel
laborers to work for less than their economic wage rate, particularly
if such legislation were combined with restrictions upon geographical mobility. Finally, a landowner might attempt to reduce his labor
costs and to increase the availability of labor by reinstating old
forms of labor service or creating new ones, at once tying the worker
to the land and obtaining his services for no more payment than
a parcel of land already in excess of supply.

It is a tribute more to the force of circumstance, perhaps, than
to the intelligence and economic rationality of the landholding
class that the agrarian history of Europe during the fourteenth and
fifteenth centuries can be told mainly in terms of such a brief list
of responses to adversity. Variation among countries during this
period was largely a matter of differences in the intensity and
prominence of specific responses among the several suggested. Some
reactions, notably those concerned with the enforcement of labor
statutes, were political rather than technological in nature, and
their use and effectiveness depended more upon the larger political
context than upon the initiative of the individual landowner. Some,
in turn, depended upon past experience, custom, and traditional
farm tenure. It is therefore necessary to explore separately the several countries and regions, remembering that even within broadly
homogeneous geographical areas, considerable diversity was always
present.

Until very recently, the agriculture of medieval England has been
studied more intensively than that of any other European country;
it is appropriate, therefore, to begin our more detailed investiga-
tions with a close examination of the nature of English agriculture
in the later Middle Ages. The complex and various responses to the
crises of the fourteenth century are most visible in England, and
even though the English patterns of climate and custom proscribed
the adoption of all of the continental solutions, the very visibility
of the English adaptations provides an apt warning against too
hasty generalization. Equally important, by considering England
at greater length than other countries, it is possible to create some
sense of the richness of detail and of the depth and interconnected-
ness of agrarian problems, which may subsequently be carried over
to the Continent, even though no simple economic model suffices to

explain all of European agriculture. In less well studied countries, the evidence may occasionally all point in the same direction, but it is not yet all in; at this juncture, we must treat it with the respectful circumspection accorded to brilliant preliminary research.

Ample English evidence exists to demonstrate the desire for, or indeed the rank necessity of, reductions in agricultural labor costs in the face of rising wages and declining cereal prices. One path that appeared open to the landowner to accomplish this end was the conversion of his tilled fields to sheep pasture. While the land remained productive, the amount of labor required could be substantially reduced. For about 40 years after the Black Death, until the last decade of the fourteenth century, the market for wool remained fairly active. The rapid development of the English cloth industry, which was only beginning to be significant at the time of the first plague, appears to have created sufficient demand for wool to keep its price high until at least the beginning of the fifteenth century. Then a sharp fall in the export levels of raw wool coincided with a precipitous decline in exports of finished woolen cloth, and wool prices inevitably sagged. In the years immediately following the Black Death, however, market conditions favored sheep farming above the cultivation of cereals, and landlords responded to the market. In one area near Oxford, for example, sheep displaced more than 30 households that had been situated in the region before the plague. Their numbers reduced first by sickness, they were, to borrow a phrase used by Sir Thomas More to describe parallel phenomena in the sixteenth century, finally consumed by the sheep. Lower labor costs and a better market for wool than for grain had rendered the older system of agriculture uneconomic and finally obsolete, along with the peasants whose services had ceased to be economically viable. The pattern of substitution of wool for grain was repeated throughout England, particularly in the Midlands, Yorkshire, and Lincolnshire, but it was by no means a universal movement.

Aside from the fact, which we shall discuss presently, that other expedients were tried in the attempt to escape the effects of the burgeoning agricultural depression, the switch to grazing was not in itself a sufficient solution to the problem. In the first place, the market for wool was not infinitely extensible; as more and more landowners transferred land to sheep grazing, both in England and on the Continent, the market inevitably weakened as the wool supply increased, and the first half of the fifteenth century witnessed falling wool prices. English wool exports declined consistently from the thirteen-nineties until midway in the fourteen-thirties they reached their lowest levels in more than a hundred years. Since cloth exports were also falling below the levels reached early in the last decade of the fourteenth century, it seems safe to conclude that the aggregate demand for English wool had fallen markedly by the first half of the fifteenth century. Although we have no figures, domestic wool consumption may possibly have increased; but it does not appear likely that the domestic demand had grown enough to absorb simultaneously the wool no longer sent overseas to continental cloth centers and the newly available wool produced by those farmers who were shifting their arable lands to pasture in search of better returns. The remedy that had promised to cure the economic ills of the landed class in the late fourteenth century was revealed by the beginning of the fifteenth century as no more than a worthless placebo. Toward the end of the latter century, conditions again improved; rising demand and prices, for both grain and wool, created antagonism among the proponents of the two alternative uses for the land, which again had become scarce. The eventual recovery of land values and agricultural prices lay in the future, beyond the period considered in the present volume, however, so we must seek further into the options chosen by the pressed landholders during their darkest hours.

In essence, the shift to wool production was only one aspect of a larger phenomenon—the attempt to produce crops the demand for which was more elastic than the demand for the basic food grains. Another such alternative crop was barley. Demand for barley was partially derived from its use as a food grain, but the more important consideration in the late fourteenth century lay in its use as the prime ingredient for the brewing of beer. Beer, of course, is a commodity that, unlike bread—despite the Wife of Bath's comparison of herself to barley bread—is consumed as much for pleasure as for its inherent nutritional value. The level of beer consumption may expand or contract over a wide range in response to its price, to changes in the consumer's level of income, and to changes in the prices of other goods. As bread prices fell, the portion of the average villager's income required for buying bread decreased, and the money saved could be spent on beer or other semi-luxury products. We may perhaps discern in addition to purely economic considerations, a psychological motivation for the increase in beer drinking that was evident in the late fourteenth century; beer is, after all, a congenial drink, whose consumption might well be expected to increase during those troubled times when the brevity of life had been made painfully and repeatedly apparent by the successive recurrences of the plague.

We need not be surprised, then, to notice an increase in the amount of brewing done in the later fourteenth century nor to observe the alacrity of the depressed agricultural sector in responding to the increased demand thus generated for barley. Where we have figures, it is possible to follow the substitution directly in the transfer of lands from the cultivation of wheat to the cultivation of barley. At Ramsey Abbey, for example, between 1340 and 1379, the proportionate share of wheat in the total output dropped by 50 per cent, while that of barley almost doubled. At Sherborne, in Gloucestershire, also, between 1425 and 1452, the share of wheat in the total production fell by half, while that of barley rose by half.

Aggregate figures, as is ever the case in the history of the Middle Ages, are lacking for the total production of barley, but specific cases confirm the general impression that barley cultivation increased relatively over the course of the fourteenth and fifteenth centuries, although this may have occurred because barley suffered a smaller absolute decline than did some of the other grains. In the absence of more satisfactory statistics, however, we must limit our judgments to estimating the relative importance of the various grains. Despite the relative increase in barley cultivation that coincided with a diminution in the share of cultivation allotted to wheat, the pattern of barley prices does not seem to have diverged significantly from the price pattern of wheat. Prices of both grains fell, but the volume of wheat sold appears, on the basis of such production statistics as there are, to have fallen further. This suggests that although the production of barley was a temporary aid to the distressed agricultural sector, the aid was, in the long run, primarily effective in providing a more extensive market rather than in restoring agricultural incomes to the older, higher levels.

Some evidence suggests that the costs of growing barley may have fallen relative to the costs of wheat farming, although the statistics are so fragmentary that considerable caution is required in their interpretation. On the estates of the Bishop of Winchester, the seed/yield ratios for both barley and wheat improve over the course of the fourteenth and fifteenth centuries, but the more significant improvement occurs in barley. On one group of estates, in the period 1400–49, the barley seed/yield ratio was 13.1 per cent higher than that pertaining in the period 1300–49; on the same basis, wheat shows no more than a 5.5 per cent increase in the return per bushel sown over the 150-year span. The differential improvement in barley yields over wheat yields is too slight and too specific to Winchester to sustain the weight of a generalized interpretation; in addition, the interpretation itself is less than clearcut. It may well be that the rising yields in both grains merely reflect the abandonment of less fertile portions of the estates; but why, then, do barley yields rise more than proportionately? Perhaps land formerly reserved for the cultivation of wheat and other crops in the rotation system was being transferred to barley culture; it is possible that such land was of a higher quality than that where barley was previously grown. Perhaps barley was simply more responsive to an improved environment than was wheat, and the relative improvement in yield was nothing more than a reflection of this fact. In any event, it does appear that on the estates of the Bishop of Winchester, at least, the cost of barley cultivation declined rather more per bushel than did the costs of production prevailing in wheat farming.

What is perfectly clear, where we have records, however, is the fact that proportionately more of the declining total acreage of arable land in England was devoted to the cultivation of barley during the late fourteenth and early fifteenth centuries than had been the case in the period prior to the first great plague; less, accordingly, was reserved for wheat. Now, since the prices of wheat and barley had declined in roughly the same proportion, it seems evident that the farmers made the correct decision by concentrating upon barley. The demand for this crop must have been more elastic, since the market was capable of absorbing relatively greater quantities of barley without more than a proportional decrease in prices. On the other hand, from the landowners' point of view, the blessings must have been rather mixed, for even though the barley market was stronger, it was not by itself capable of sustaining agricultural incomes at the pre-plague level. The landlords had chosen the best course of action in shifting to barley, but the choice was among options to minimize losses rather than to increase gains.

Related to barley and an agricultural product with high demand elasticity, stock raising—the provision of meat and poultry and the production of such farm commodities as cheese, butter, and eggs—gave the landholding class another alternative for the internal shifting of productive assets in the endeavor to find some respite from the declining revenues of the more traditional grain crops. To some extent, the shift of emphasis favoring stock raising in the later Middle Ages supported the market for barley, since, aside from its importance as the prime ingredient in beer making, barley also served as a fodder crop and hence as one of the raw materials needed for the production of dairy goods and meat. By the same token, several of the other grains that served as fodder benefited from the demand derived from their use as secondary goods in stock raising. Oats, although to a lesser degree, and various legumes, primarily peas, show the most striking development in this category. At Leicester Abbey, for example, the importance of peas in the total receipts only slightly less than doubled between 1363 and 1401; at Ramsey Abbey, the share of legumes increased from 16 per cent in 1307 to 44 per cent in 1379.[5] Now, the increase in the share allotted to legumes in the total production may have had important effects upon the attainable output levels of other crops. Legumes are significant sources of valuable soil nitrogen and, when included in a system of crop rotation, even for reasons unrelated to scientific agronomy, they will serve to enrich the land. Thus it is possible that the evidence of rising soil productivity in some regions will have to be explained not only in terms of the abandonment of marginal lands, but also in terms of a better balanced, if accidental, system of crop rotation. Further, in addition to providing nitrogen, the allocation of more land to fodder crops allows the land to carry

    [5] J. A. Raftis, *The Estates of Ramsey Abbey. A Study in Economic Growth and Organization* (Toronto, 1957).

larger herds, and this in its turn again supplements soil productivity as a result of the increased availability of animal manure. Needless to say, a parallel effect may appear as a result of the expansion of sheep farming.

We have already noted the improvement in barley yields at Winchester and have observed their relative gain over wheat yields. In the case of oats, a fodder crop, the improvement in yield is even more pronounced; at Winchester, the average yield per bushel of seed during the period 1400–49 was at least 50 per cent greater than that attained in the period 1300–49. Elsewhere in England the seed/yield ratio seems to have doubled. Where there is evidence, however, the number of acres devoted to this crop appear to have fallen considerably, although not so sharply as the wheat acreage. Because of the improved yields, the significance of oats in the total production appears, on the contrary, to have risen on a number of the Bishop of Winchester's manors during the late fourteenth and early fifteenth centuries.

Statistics on the yield of peas, perhaps the most important of the fodder crops, are too fragmentary to allow any firm conclusions regarding productivity; for this crop, the yield aspects of agricultural history must remain essentially a blank page until further research is accomplished. In the cultivation of oats and barley, however, it appears that farmers benefited from substantially lower relative costs of production in comparison with wheat, although it must be remembered that seed/yield ratios are a very complex measure, abstracted as they are from labor and land costs. In any event, if we allow the economist's Panglossian condition of all other things being equal, the landholder could grow oats and barley at relatively lower costs than wheat as the fourteenth and fifteenth centuries progressed.

In addition, the demand for oats, peas, and barley as fodder in all probability rendered the cultivation of these crops more desirable than wheat from the market side as well. In some cases, however, as on the seignorial estates at Ramsey Abbey, the evidence contradicts this proposition, indicating either that the landlords did not take advantage of the market or that there were special factors at work on these estates. We have suggested above that lower bread prices freed a portion of the incomes of the nonfarming classes for the purchase of such modest luxuries as beer; it is equally true that the newly available spending power could be directed toward a more general improvement of diet and toward the introduction of such commodities as meat and butter.

Empirical evidence suggests that this was the case; both of these commodities exhibit price patterns which are sharply differentiated from those of the basic grains. Instead of falling, the price of meat in England actually rose in monetary terms, although this rise is in large part vitiated when account is taken of the several debasements of the coinage which weakened the value of money. Debasement, however, affects the value of the money used for all products equally; so the fact remains that meat, which even after adjustment for the monetary mutations, held close to its pre-plague price levels, was a more attractive product for the landholders to raise than wheat. Butter presents virtually the same market pattern as meat, generally maintaining its old price level and indeed, in some cases, even rising above the old levels, expressed in real terms.

We thus far have touched only upon the demand elasticities of meat and butter without attempting to consider the factors that affected their supply. To explain the price stability evident in these commodities, both sides of the market must be taken into account. Our information is too limited and too imprecise to allow firm conclusions, but it is revealing to consider some of the economic conditions that could have affected the size of herds and the growing of livestock, even though we cannot then convert our speculations into firm historical fact. In the first place, Malthus to the contrary, in an economy where land has become surplus, the cereal crops may be expanded very readily so long as there is labor available that may be transferred from other occupations. On the other hand, the natural process of animal reproduction has obvious upper limits in the short run, and it is not possible to increase the herds so rapidly as one may extend the arable land. Herds grow slowly in the best of times, but the fourteenth century was not the best of times; cattle murrains struck the English flocks and herds throughout the century and major epizootics occurred in the years 1348, 1363, and 1369. Further, if the purpose of herding is to provide meat for the market, it is obvious that the rate of growth of the herd is inversely proportional to variations in the level of sales. In addition, the size of

herds was in all probability loosely correlated with the human
death rate, since one of the traditional forms of payment for heriots,
or death duties, was the best beast on the holding. The collecting
landlord, already faced by problems of declining revenues and decreasing sources of labor, might readily seek to convert these heriot
payments into cash, rather than to keep them as an augmentation
of his own grazing stock. Thus, a demographic crisis among humans
might produce a parallel catastrophe in the animal kingdom and
set back the potential growth rate of the herds, despite all the economic inducements urging their expansion. Historically, there appears to have been something of a short-term glut on the London
meat market in the years immediately following the Black Death,
as landlords attempted to convert animals received as death taxes or
entry fines into cash.

Landholders who had switched to stock raising benefited to the
degree that the slow natural rate of increase of herds sustained the
price of meat, but the benefit was limited by precisely the same
factors that created it. Because herds were held within bounds imposed by physiological limitations upon reproduction and by the
economic pressure upon landlords, faced by declining revenues in
other sectors, to slaughter their animals for the market, the price of
meats remained high, but the stock raiser could expand neither his
herds nor his sales as much as he might have wished. Meat prices,
then, are not by themselves an index of the total revenue derived
from herding. The crucial factor is, of course, the product of the
price times the quantity sold, and with this in mind, it seems clear
that even such a pocket of prosperity as the active meat market
could not suffice to replace the revenues lost from the traditional
grain crops.

Even within the stock-raising segment of agriculture, certain economic forces were at work to counterbalance the enhanced profitability of meat production. Complementarity of production is a well
known phenomenon even today; a cold winter will force oil refiners
to produce more fuel oil and hence more gasoline as a by-product,
thus lowering the summer price of the latter. Total profits will depend upon both products. In the same fashion, in the fourteenth
and fifteenth centuries, increased consumption of meat tended to
create a surplus of the by-product hides and hence to lower the

price of that commodity. Since hides were a major English export and a significant cash crop, the negative effect of a fall in hide prices upon the total profitability of stock raising must not be overlooked. Measured in shillings of account, the average price of hides at Winchester in the 50-year period following the Black Death was more than 32 per cent below that prevailing in the period 1260–1350. After adjustment for the debasement of the coinage during the latter half of the century, the decrease in the average price of hides grows to almost 50 per cent. Again, the pattern of limited success in meeting the crisis in the aggregate revenues of the agricultural sector emerges. The correct action, in terms of economics, was indeed taken by those who turned to stock raising, but the result was merely to maximize revenues at lower levels, not to increase profits nor even to maintain them.

To this point, we have emphasized those problems which faced landholders who farmed their lands on their own behalf despite the increasing difficulties. An alternative response to diminishing profit that was distinct from the internal shifts among crops and factors of production was simply to abandon the attempt to farm the demesne, to rent out the land at the best possible rate even if it were very low, and to concentrate productive resources elsewhere, either on smaller, more viable holdings or in some form of rural industry less susceptible to the general malaise of the agricultural sector. Leasing rather than directly cultivating the demesne land was neither unique to the fourteenth century, nor did it proceed at a demonstrably greater rate during this period. It tended rather to be a continuous pattern from the middle of the thirteenth century, but within the long-term trend itself, there was an internal and dynamic mechanism, forcing its continuance and converting it into an economic trap for the landlords of the later Middle Ages. As the labor services of earlier times were commuted to money rents, the semiservile labor available for the cultivation of the demesne lands declined, and demesne cultivation came to depend more and more upon the employment of casual, hired labor during the peak seasons of agricultural activity. When the population was severely reduced by disease and plague during the latter half of the fourteenth century, this source of labor waned at the same time as the market forces described above rendered agriculture less profitable, even if labor had been available at the old rates. With land surplus in terms of the demand for the products of the soil, and labor scarce, many landlords—some partially, some totally—abandoned direct cultivation of their demesne lands and put them out to lease, thus putting pressure upon on the land market and causing sharp reductions in rents. When land was available and cheap, several new economic linkages developed that further worsened the position of the landlord.

In the first place, as the market for land was very thin, the potential tenant was in a position to shop around for the most favorable terms. Quite naturally, tenants sought to avoid lands burdened with onerous labor services and to bargain for unencumbered lands at low rents. On one English estate in the quarter-century following the plague, the landlord was compelled to take back almost three-quarters of the holdings which he had let out subject to labor services. We may observe that by subtracting additional quantities of labor from the already scarce supply, the large-scale loss of tenants who owed labor services further increased the problem inherent in the direct cultivation of the demesne by the lord of the manor. This in turn would accelerate and encourage the already evident tendency to rent out demesne lands and, at the same time, by increasing the availability of land, enhance the bargaining position of potential tenants. This vicious circle is in itself complete, but a second, related set of circumstances was also present. The existence of land at low rents enabled those sub-subsistence farmers whose holdings were too small to provide adequate support for themselves and their families to increase the size of their farms on highly favorable terms. In one abbey, the average size of holdings more than doubled between the early fourteenth century and the middle of the fifteenth. The economic effect of the increase in the average acreage of small farms was inevitably twofold. On the one hand, as the relative number of farms below the subsistence level decreased, the supply of day labor decreased, but by a greater proportion than would have resulted from the population decline alone. On the other hand, as farms grew in size, fewer families in the agricultural sector were compelled to come into the market to supplement their domestic food supplies, and thus the aggregate demand for grain fell. Again, the downward pressure on the larger landholders' revenues is visible. As small holdings grew in size, more labor was required at home, and consequently less—and more expensive—labor was available to the greater landlords, who were producing for a thinner, weaker market. Each time a landlord was driven to rent out more land, he thereby further undermined his economic position by making rents lower, grain cheaper, and labor more expensive.

The forces that had caused land values and rents to rise and marginal lands to become economically valuable during the course of the thirteenth century were in large part absent after the middle of the following century. In the absence of labor to work the land and of markets in which to sell agricultural products, the marginal productivity of land, given the extent of arable in existence prior to the demographic crises, fell to zero in the latter portion of the fourteenth century. Nothing the landlord nor even the state could do was capable of altering this hard economic fact. Rents continued to fall, and some, particularly those that lay in the former wheat-producing areas of the east of England, ultimately reached zero simultaneously with the marginal product of the land. When this happened, those lands had ceased to be economic goods and hence ceased to justify the expense involved in plowing and keeping down the weeds and scrub growth. Landlords consequently allowed, or rather were forced to allow, arable acreage to revert either to pasture or simply to waste. Presumably, some selectivity was exercised in determining which lands to abandon; the more costly and less productive lands probably dropped out of cultivation first, but the scale of the reversion of arable was so great that not all the abandoned lands could have been marginal in terms of soil fertility alone. In the hundred years following the first occurrence of the Black Death, some 450 large English villages simply disappeared, along with a great many smaller ones. Duby calculates that this loss represented approximately one-fifteenth of the total rural units extant in England in 1300.[6] Since the loss was more concentrated in some regions than in others, considerable caution is indicated before we assume, as certain scholars have done, that soil productivity was everywhere improved. The less specific deduction that the net economic return

[6] Georges Duby, *Rural Economy and Country Life in the Medieval West* (Columbia: University of South Carolina Press, 1968).

per acre of the remaining lands was greater than that of the abandoned lands is more sound, however, since it simultaneously com-
prehends soil fertility, shifts in the organization of the fields, market location, and the suitability of the remaining lands for the
production of those crops with high or higher demand elasticity
than cereals.

Since the shortage of labor was so great that land had to be abandoned, it did not require a vast leap of the landlords' imagination
for them to conclude that something ought to be done to assure
their labor supplies and to increase, or at least to hold constant, the
number of tenants. One direct course of action for obtaining this
end was the rather general attempt to revive the old labor services
—plowing, threshing, carting, and harvesting, to name a few—that
had fallen into desuetude on many estates during the century preceding the plague. Here, however, was an action that moved in direct opposition to the economic foundations and forces prevailing
in the later Middle Ages. Each new disaster suffered by the landlords enhanced the bargaining position of the peasants, so that attempts to resuscitate obsolete feudal burdens were foredoomed to
failure. No single landlord had the strength to repress peasant labor
against the power of such generalized economic pressures. Indeed,
it seems that the greater landholders, whether more circumspect or
more hopeless, exhibited less vigor in this regard than those smaller
holders who often had only recently acquired control of the land as
a result of the troubles of the great.

The smaller landlords, weaker than the great lords in both political and economic power and incapable, by themselves, of acting in
concert, sought remedies for their economic problems by turning to
the central government, that is, to the more national power of the
king and parliament. The Ordinance of 1349 and then the Statute
of Laborers of 1351 attempted to answer the needs of landholders
by limiting wages to pre-plague levels, by forcing work at those
rates upon all men less than 60 years old, and by restricting the mobility of labor through provisions that decreed that the territorial
lord had the first claim on labor services and that declared the hiring of workers who abandoned their former masters a criminal act.
The Cambridge Statute of 1388 was even more repressive; its desperate tone indicates the failure of earlier legislation. Here one

finds labor mobility forbidden without written permission from the local justices, and there is even an attempt to legislate enforced child labor in agriculture. The enactment of more such legislation, though not usually so harsh, continues into the fifteenth century with a regularity that confirms what we know from other sources as well: no amount of legislation could reverse the tide that was carrying away the profits of English landholders.

In part, failure came because the opportunity cost to a peasant of remaining on the land at the old wages was too high to be tolerated. As landlords found that they could not obtain workers at the arbitrary wages set by the law, they tended to compete among themselves and hence to destroy the effectiveness of the wage legislation initiated in their interest. Within the propertied class itself, some landlords were in a stronger position than others; larger holders possessed a competitive edge over their smaller counterparts and hence they were less eager to abide by rules that favored the small landlord by equalizing access to labor. Enterprising peasants, therefore, found little difficulty in evading the statutes, since it was in the direct interest of the powerful to aid them in subverting the law. Wages inevitably rose as restrictions on labor mobility collapsed. Nor was competition for labor limited to the agricultural sector alone; the demand for manufactured products was more elastic than that for agricultural goods, and the industrial sector consequently exercised a strong pull upon the services of available workers. Flight from the land became common despite all efforts to prevent it; laws were multiplied and reiterated but to no avail. In 1406, almost 60 years after the first great plague, statutes were still being enacted to stem the exodus of peasants from the soil. Their chief effect was to document the failure of earlier legislation to prevent disaster.

In some cases, landholders learned to sway with the economic winds and to try to capitalize upon the demand for manufactured goods, just as some had switched from cereals to commodities exhibiting greater demand elasticity. The fourteenth and fifteenth centuries in England were the age of rural industry. Some scholars have written of the fifteenth century as a period of industrial growth on English manors, but the evidence of growth on any large scale is particularly cloudy, limited to a few regions, and often closely tied to the wartime needs of the monarchy. The existence of an occasional and outstanding war profiteer such as Sir John Fastolf, who drew substantial revenues from the clothworkers on his estates, is not enough to prove that manorholders all over England had met their economic difficulties by renting their lands to nascent industrialists. Rather, one might view Sir John's success in cloth manufacturing as a sign of the wider failure of agricultural profits; the prosperity of his estates at Castle Combe derived from their location and the presence of water power, not from the land. These advantages could not be duplicated at will in all regions, as the receipts from a number of other manors will indicate. The revenues of the Bishop of Durham dropped by more than half between 1308 and 1373; by 1446, they had fallen to one-third their earlier level. An exact parallel existed on the Percy estates in Sussex, and declines of almost the same magnitude may be observed in Forncett and Wilburton. Whereas some few fortunate landlords may have found profit in rural industries and fewer still have recouped their economic fortunes within the agricultural sector itself, the overriding picture was one of gloom. Defensive measures provided some relief, an occasional outstanding success brightened the darkness of the rural economy, but the position of the landlords continued to deteriorate during the late fourteenth and early fifteenth centuries.

What was the position, however, of the peasants and of the very small landholders? Did not their status rise as their bargaining power grew? Do not the vultures grow fat when the lions starve? To seek answers to these questions, among the most difficult in economic history because of the absence of records concerning the peasants, it is necessary to separate peasant activity into three categories; the peasant may be viewed as a subsistence farmer, as a producer of cash crops for the market, and as a casual laborer working for others. The events of the fourteenth and fifteenth centuries had quite different, often divergent, effects upon each of these activities. In his role as subsistence farmer, there can be little doubt that the lot of the peasant improved; land was cheaper and conditions of tenure less burdensome. Further, the availability of numerous and varied holdings at low rents probably enabled the peasant to select more fertile land or at least to rationalize his holdings so as to reduce such personal and economic costs as resulted from travel among widely scattered fields. He may also have found that additional space, by enabling him to raise limited quantities of livestock for his own consumption, gave him more opportunity to vary his diet. From a number of influences, then, the peasant's diet probably improved, and his income, measured in caloric intake rather than in money, grew. On the other hand, if he attempted to grow economically beyond the minimum level of household sub-sistence, he faced the identical problems that afflicted the larger landlords. Labor was as scarce, and markets were as thin, for the en-terprising peasant as they were for the great lord, while the lesser sophistication and power of the peasant rendered him if anything more vulnerable to the economic setbacks common to a period of declining markets. It does not seem likely, therefore, that many peasants successfully rose to wealth during the hundred years or so following the great plague. In the long run, however, the first up-ward steps toward wealth may have been taken during this period. The strategic position of the small holder improved, so that when land values rose and market conditions improved toward the end of the fifteenth century, certain peasant families could traverse the border between subsistence and the dynamic accumulation of wealth. For our period, however, the limitations upon peasant growth were very narrow; improvement in diet, consequently, is more perceptible than improvement in monetary income. Even in the later period, only the lucky few found their fortunes, while the great majority either slid back or merely managed to hold firm to their modest status.

There is evidence that precisely those factors which contributed to dietary improvements tended to reduce monetary income. Wage rates indeed rose, but wage rates are not a measure of income unless they are refined by knowledge of the number of days worked and of the levels of employment. Such information is simply unavailable for the later Middle Ages, but certain circumstantial material per-mits us to draw some inferences in this regard. The constant com-plaints about the scarcity of labor and the frequent enunciation of new laws to bind labor to the agricultural sector in a period of de-clining markets suggest that advancing wages were not correlated with increased employment. Growth in the size of small holdings probably worsened the labor shortage, since the increased area freed many peasants from the necessity of seeking supplemental earnings and simultaneously absorbed substantial quantities of labor in self-employment on personal holdings. This, in its turn, would have served to reduce money incomes among the lowest ranks of rural society, creating the somewhat anomalous situation in which welfare, by our definition, may have risen in conjunction with falling monetary income.

The question of peasant welfare is one of the more fiery controversies current among medieval economic historians. To some extent, the flames are fanned by modern political bias. Writers from the leftist camp have tended to view the easing of labor services, the improvement in the size of holdings, and the nutritional gains of the peasantry as signs of economic growth and affluence, of the defeat of a rather ill-defined feudalism, and of the triumph of the exploited class. On the other side, scholars have contraposed the dismal position of the landlords, the declining revenues of manors, failures in the monetary portion of the agricultural sector, and certain trade figures, which we will examine subsequently. The issue is delicate and no clear resolution is likely in the present state of our knowledge; in part, the problem rests upon the definition of terms and of the relative weights assigned to the various sectors of society in measuring prosperity or its absence. Partly, too, the discussion entails certain assumptions, rarely explicitly stated, regarding the peasants' conception of the determinants of their own welfare and of the value system upon which it was based. It is probably true that the average peasant had more bread to eat in the late than in the early fourteenth century, but it is a maxim of economics, albeit a borrowed one, that man cannot live by bread alone. The peasant's chances of selling cash crops were reduced by the economic circumstances of the post-plague era, while at the same time the prices of manufactured goods rose. As a result, the peasant was caught in a trap—squeezed between his falling earnings and the rising costs of goods he could not produce himself—so that if he measured his welfare in terms of his access to the market economy, we may presume that he was, if anything, somewhat worse off. To the degree that materials purchased from the nonagricultural sector of the economy were important to the peasant, his welfare, measured subjectively, must have fallen. The issue remains cloudy, however, and considerable caution is necessary in formulating even a tentative judgment.

From another point of view—the peasant's own—we may perhaps find a further witness to his condition. In this context, we must again recall the numerous attempts to bind the laborer to the soil, to prevent him from fleeing to cities or towns, and to force him to work. At the first level, it would appear obvious that conditions in the agricultural economy were not so attractive to the peasant that he wished to remain on the land and enjoy a rising status. At the second level, the numerous and newly introduced laws, designed to constrain the peasant and even to force his children to work, must have exerted a negative effect upon his well-being. We should bear in mind, also, that the constraints had come to be exercised by a new and more impersonal authority, one that consequently was free at once from the traditional limits imposed by custom and from the mitigating influence of interpersonal relationships. The necessities of war finance rendered the repressive labor laws even less palatable; rights of purveyance, forced sales to the government at low prices, and increased taxation such as the series of poll taxes in the late thirteen-seventies further inflamed peasant sentiment against the intrusion in rural affairs of the central government on a novel scale.

The response of the peasantry was also on a new scale. In 1381, prompted by the imposition of the national poll tax at the very high rates required to meet the expenses of the Hundred Years' War after a period of brilliant French victories, the peasants rose throughout all of England, one group marching on London to threaten Richard II, then a boy of fourteen. The demands made— abolition of villenage, freedom of labor, specifically an end to the various new labor laws, and demands for even cheaper and more easily available land—reiterate the fact that not all was well in the rural economy. Those who wish to depict the late fourteenth century in England as a period in which the peasant made substantial gains should be careful not to underestimate the very real economic and political problems afflicting him. In the long run, the groundwork for progress may have been established at this time, but in the short run, low agricultural prices, high costs, increased taxation, and repressive labor laws did much, in my opinion, to cancel any immediate gain derived from the increased availability of land.

France

The agricultural situation in England was not dissimilar to conditions observable throughout northwestern Europe. Details, of course, vary from region to region, but the problems posed by the economic crisis of the later Middle Ages were everywhere similar; the intensity of the dislocations differed, as did the potential for finding remedies and palliatives. In France, for example, beyond the purely economic factors afflicting agriculture, military defeat and the political disruption induced by the Hundred Years' War caused considerable damage over wide areas of the country. The periodic English invasions, whether sweeping down from Flanders and passing south of Paris or moving eastward from the English-held Bordeaux region, invariably were coupled with attempts to devastate the fields and crops lying along the route. Already suffering from the ills common to landholders everywhere, the French were further burdened by the costs of war. It is well, however, at least for the fourteenth century, not to overemphasize these costs; armies were small—usually 5,000 to 10,000 men—and the destruction they could cause was therefore limited. Indeed, in the early thirteen-seventies, the brilliant French constable Bertrand Du Guesclin founded his military strategy upon this knowledge. By withdrawing into enclosed and fortified cities and refusing to fight save on his own terms, he was able to inflict more harm upon the English than had been accomplished in open warfare. Natural forces and the weakness of medieval supply lines defeated the English more effectively than did the French knights. In a period of about five years, Du Guesclin managed to reconquer almost all of the English holdings in southwestern France. For the strategy of waiting and avoiding pitched battles to succeed, one precondition was necessary; the damage wreaked by the English could not be of long duration. France could endure the regional loss of one year's crops, particularly during a time of relative grain surplus, so long as the following year's crops were adequate; once the enemy troops had passed, the ground could be sown again, and recovery was normally swift, if not without substantial hardship and violent but temporary dislocation of the grain markets.

Medieval agricultural technique was simple, and primitive or semiprimitive methodology was in fact advantageous when the issue was resistance to war. The earth itself could not be destroyed even though the corps were burned, and the low levels of capital investment meant low vulnerability to armed attack. Simple tools could easily be concealed; if they were demolished, they could easily be remade. Not everything in the agricultural sector was indestructible, however, and some segments of the rural economy were more vulnerable than others. Livestock and beasts of burden were normally hustled away from the path of the invaders, but mistakes occurred. When herds and draft animals were destroyed, the recovery rate was far slower than was the case with scorched fields. Moreover, since draft animals were capital goods, their loss had a cumulative effect upon future grain production. Large-scale capital investment also existed in the form of mills, barns, and manor houses, all of which were subject to the torches of the English, and since loot was more likely to be found among the wealthy landlords, marauding soldiers turned their attention to precisely those religious and noble houses where capital investment was large, expensive, and difficult to replace. Among the crops themselves, some suffered more than others; wheat might grow again within one year, but the destruction of vineyards and orchards was a more serious loss, requiring, as was the case with livestock, a period of years to overcome.

In the long run, the immediate passage of the occasional English armies probably did far less harm than the resultant breakdown of the political order within France itself. Following the French defeat at the battle of Poitiers in 1356, large numbers of soldiers—English and French mercenaries, and foreign adventurers—were released from military service and consequently left without money or means of support. Trained only for war, and living in a period of political chaos, the disbanded soldiers formed into armed groups and collectively sought careers as professional bandits. They naturally sought to plunder those regions which would yield the richest booty and thus, like locusts, they fanned out over France, pillaging those areas that had previously escaped the pains of war and the passage of the English. The devastation was more complete, since the bandits, or *routiers,* were more ubiquitous than the English, could vary their routes more widely, and did not elicit even the modest defensive military effort the French directed against their national enemy. The problem of the *routiers* remained endemic throughout the entire Hundred Years' War (1337–1453) in France, sometimes becoming less virulent under a strong king such as Charles V (1364–80), who managed to export many of them as soldiers in his Spanish campaign. The problem always returned, however, with each new military effort, and it became more serious with the passage of time, as the pressures of war and misrule broke down political order in France.

The agricultural economy, then, was afflicted not only by falling prices for the traditional grains but also by growing political insecurity. Less is known about French than English agricultural history during this period, and the incalculable impact of the war makes each judgment more complex, but such evidence as there is reveals considerable similarity to developments in England and Germany. In some regions, notably Brie, fields were abandoned, and agricultural villages disappeared. Price patterns, after adjustments have been made for the very frequent mutations of the coinage, show roughly the same trends as are evident for England, but spasms of war-induced scarcity disrupted the smoothness of the trend. In a single year, for example, regional wheat prices may show an eight- to tenfold rise in response to local adversities, crop failure, war, or the activities of the raiding *routiers.*

It is certain that conditions on the land were less secure in France than in England during the late fourteenth and early fifteenth centuries. It is equally clear that those who were able to do so sought the comparative safety of the cities and towns. In a period of war and disorder, it is no wonder that many landlords preferred the security of an urban dwelling to the risky isolation of a country house where the least sign of comfort or affluence acted as a beacon light to attract booty-hungry marauders. The movement of landlords from the land inevitably increased the economic difficulties already induced by the fall in grain prices; money paid as rent to landlords who had become urban dwellers did not return to the rural sector, and lower prices made such rent money ever more difficult to earn. Landlords found that in many areas investmnt on their estates entailed great risk and small profit; so even this source of funds for the rural sector tended to dry up. Under these conditions, something of a balance-of-payments crisis must have developed between the countryside and the towns, constantly draining money away from the rural economy.

The flow of funds from rural areas was intensified by the growing exigencies of royal finance. When the French king, Jean le Bon, was captured by the English in 1356, his ransom was set at 3,000,000 *écus* of gold, and an extensive tax structure was devised to meet the payments. The ransom was never entirely paid, but despite a brief respite during the tax revolts in 1381, the new and increased taxes became permanent. The most important of these taxes was the *taille,* a direct levy on non-noble property, and consequently a direct blow against the already shaky position of the overburdened peasantry. Tax-exempt nobles, by collecting rents and living in the towns, drew money from the agricultural economy; the central government, by collecting the *taille,* did the same. Since investment was reduced by fear of war and political insecurity, and since the demand for basic food grains had declined as a result of demographic losses, there was little opportunity for the French rural economy to earn enough cash to meet its increased burdens. The rural sector was thus slowly impoverished, and as the fourteenth and early fifteenth centuries progressed, rents inevitably fell, drawn down by combined economic and fiscal pressures. Ultimately, the landlords' returns declined sharply, and as in England, lands were abandoned and fields were allowed to revert to pasture or waste.

Although investment in the land was risky and no longer directed along the traditional paths, it was not nonexistent. As in the case of England, some crops weathered the economic storms of the late fourteenth and early fifteenth centuries better than others; demand for them either increased or remained high enough to strain the reduced capacities for production. In contrast to the English, French townspeople tended to invest on a rather significant scale in the purchase of lands located near the cities and to use their investments both as a source of revenue and as a guarantee against famine. Wisdom dictated, of course, that agricultural investment be made in those crops which displayed the greatest resilience to market disruptions; consequently, money was spent primarily in the purchase of lands given to crops with high demand elasticity. In France, wine assumed the role that barley held elsewhere. Everywhere, during the later Middle Ages, per capita wine consumption appears to have risen as consumers, benefiting from lower bread prices, were able to shift a portion of their food budgets into more luxurious amenities of the table. In England, not a wine-producing country, wine prices doubled over the course of the fourteenth century, and in many areas of France, as in the Dauphiné, producers expanded the vineyards to meet the rising demands. There is evidence that in other areas, such as the region around Toulouse, however, wine production could not stand the pressure of the higher labor costs that followed the plagues; in these areas, the number of vines may have contracted. Despite occasional local instances of contraction, there remains a general impression of an expansion in vineyards or at least of an expansion in the proportion of the agricultural output allocated to wine.

Another word of caution is advisable at this point; although the Black Death precipitated very rapid reallocation of fields and crops, one must not overdramatize its effects nor view it as the ultimate cause of all the economic changes visible in the later Middle Ages. As early as the famine of 1315–17, signs of change and of shifts among various crops were apparent. One Cistercian monastery, Veulerent, in Central France, was already increasing the amount of land given over to vines at that time. In addtion, land, increasingly let out for money rents and no longer cultivated by the monks, was being converted to the production of other, more specialized industrial crops. The quantity of land in sheep pasture increased to supply the needs of the woolen industry, and at the same time, a significant portion of the rented lands was devoted to the cultivation of woad, one of the most important medieval dyestuffs. Despite their efforts to increase revenues and to adjust to the vicissitudes of the fourteenth-century economy, the monks at Veulerent discovered, as did most English landholders, that they were fighting against insuperable odds. The steps taken to maintain revenue were the correct ones, but in the long run they failed, and income continued to fall. By the fifteenth century, the monastery had virtually ceased to be an operating farm; the immense grange, built to store grain during the prosperous thirteenth century, had become a gutted casualty of the Hundred Years' War.

In France, as in England, the rural economic landscape was mottled rather than totally dark; some segments, notably those producing wine, fared better; some, particularly those wheatlands and manors which fell victim to pillage by soldiers or bandits, fared far worse than any comparable holdings in England. At the lowest social levels, among the peasants, the same forces were at work in both countries. French peasants benefited from the enhanced accessibility of land, from their improved bargaining position as laborers, and from lighter tenure burdens as leaseholders. They suffered as much from repressive labor measures, and much more than their English counterparts from the scourges of war and of the *routiers*. In addition, it is likely that the tax burden they shouldered was substantially larger than that levied against the English peasants; revolt among the peasants was, after all, at least as intense in France as in England and came more swiftly. The revolt of the Jacquerie (Jacques was a common peasant name) of the thirteenfifties was an early statement of agrarian discontent. It was followed in 1379–83 by the spiraling series of rural and urban uprisings that were directed against the taxes imposed by Charles V and mismanaged after his death. Even though their status may have improved in certain limited aspects, the French peasants were no more satisfied with their lot than were their brothers across the Channel. Two factors probably worsened the comparative position of the Frenchman: taxation was almost certainly more onerous in France; secondly, however, the interest of the French townsman in the land, in conjunction with taxation at high levels, may have interacted to crush the peasant. Taxation imposed a need for liquid money at regular intervals during a period when market conditions had rendered the acquisition of cash increasingly difficult for members of the rural economy. Peasants, therefore, were compelled to turn to the towns to raise funds, either through loans or through what amounted to forced sales of their produce. In either case, the bargaining position of the peasant was extremely weak. It did not take long for the shrewd, urban bourgeoisie to learn to capitalize upon this weakness, further reducing the peasants' position and drawing them under the tutelage of the towns. Thus, instead of gaining freedom, many French peasants simply changed masters; freed from the reciprocal ties of economic feudalism, they were bound anew by the one-sided and often harsher ties imposed through the control of monetary credit.

Germany

In Germany, as in France and England, the agricultural crisis of the fourteenth and fifteenth centuries caused major dislocations in rural society. The pattern of land abandonment, apparent elsewhere, occurred on a massive scale in Germany; in some portions of Thuringia, more than 80 per cent of the villages that had existed in the thirteenth century had disappeared by the fifteenth. Prices for grains fell sharply, and during the fourteenth century, labor became scarce as the demographic crises at once thinned the population and reduced the flow of immigrants from other areas. As elsewhere in Europe, alternative crops were substituted for grain as landlords and farmers attempted to find products the demand for which remained reasonably high. Wine, as in France, was one such crop, and viticulture assumed an increasingly important role in the agrarian economy of southern Germany. To the west, the cultivation of flax, the raw material of the linen industry, offered landholders some relief from the pressure of declining grain prices, since the consumption of cloth was not limited, as was that of grain, by physically determinate appetites. In the central portions of Germany (Franconia and Thuringia) the cultivation of dyestuffs increased during the fourteenth century in another, but probably only marginally successful, attempt to shift to crops where demand was better sustained than in the case of cereals. In some instances, the high cost of labor and the low price of grain led landholders to specialize in that form of agriculture which required the lowest possible labor input; fields were allowed to revert to woodland, and timber ultimately became the chief product of such lands. Land in those regions had fallen to such low values that it became economically feasible to allow it to lie idle during the extended period of time necessary for the development of a forest. In this interim, what returns there were came mostly from swineherding and loosing pigs in the forest to seek acorns for fodder. Pork held its price level better than grain and it seems that with labor expensive and land cheap, the conversion of arable fields to woodlands was economically rational. It does not appear plausible to assume that the resultant system yielded anything like the profits extracted from cereal cultivation under the more favorable conditions of the late thirteenth century.

North German agriculture may have fared a little better than the general pattern; there is evidence, for example, that fewer villages disappeared from this region than in the area to the east and the immediate south, where land that had been occupied during the population expansion of the thirteenth century was too marginal in character to be cultivated during the period of contraction. Perhaps, too, the expanding power of the Hanseatic league in Scandinavia contributed to the resilience of the north by opening a new market for German grain and beer. At least from the thirteenth century on, Norway had been dependent on wheat imports in order to feed a population that earned its living through trade, fishing, and specialized agriculture such as stock raising and dairy farming. England had been the traditional supplier during the high Middle Ages, but by the late thirteenth century, she had lost her exclusive role, although her exports were still important. By the middle of the fourteenth century, the English were virtually excluded. Perhaps the scarcity of labor in England and the growth in size of small holdings, by partially demonetizing the rural economy and thus reducing the market-oriented segment of English agriculture, had further diminished the slight surplus available for export. Perhaps, also, the events associated with the outbreak of the Hundred Years' War limited the supply of commercial shipping. Naval power was almost certainly diverted by the necessity of convoying the Gascon wine ships after 1336, by the requirements of the fleet at the victorious battle of Sluys off the Flemish coast in 1340, and by the subsequent continental victories and the siege of Calais. In any event, in 1343, the Hanse merchants established a trading counter at Bergen, in Norway, and managed over the next thirty years virtually to exclude English traders through a successful drive to obtain commercial dominance in the north. By 1400, just under 25 per cent of the population of Bergen was German.

Scandinavia

Conditions for cereal cultivation in Norway were poor; the climate was cold and over much of the region, the three-field system was impractical. At best, grain growing could be carried on only when grain was very dear on the international market and when import costs were correspondingly high. Clearly, these conditions were not present in the latter half of the fourteenth century: falling grain prices in Germany made imported wheat and rye cheaper than domestically grown grain. Norwegian farmers, faced with the new external competition, ceased to be competitive; grain prices fell, rents collapsed, and farmers abandoned the land to find other occupations. In the long run, the German agrarian crisis, by reducing the price of grain, gave the Hanse towns an opportunity to extend their control over the Norwegians. Once Norwegian cereal farming was destroyed and the Germans safely ensconced in the grain trade, the Hanse towns, by withholding shipments, could use their economic power in order to turn the commercial balance in their favor by starving Norway. Control of the grain trade enabled German merchants to regulate the prices paid to Norwegian hunters and fishermen; by extending credit on grain purchases, they could compound the bondage through the pressure of debt. So successful was this policy that the Germans, by the early fifteenth century, could claim total hegemony over international shipping at Bergen, limiting the number of non-German ships and regulating the sale of the goods carried, so that they had the right to purchase goods first and at wholesale prices. Thus, as we shall show more fully later on, the agrarian crisis bestowed substantial, if derivative, benefits upon German trade.

Initially, the Scandinavian concentration upon specialized agricultural products seemed to be a highly rational economic strategy. Swedish butter found a large and profitable market during the late fourteenth century when butter prices rose all over Europe; lower bread prices freed funds for the purchase of butter, while the very low milk and butterfat yields per cow, less than one-third those in modern times, limited the supply. In Norway, the value of the fish trade grew at a brisk rate in the second half of the century, constituting some 90 per cent of the export trade of Bergen. Fish prices, paralleling those of butter, held high levels as consumers substituted fish for a portion of the starch formerly contained in their diets. In this case, however, it is well to recall that it was the German traders at Bergen who controlled the export trade and thus undoubtedly gleaned the greater share of the profits.

Central Europe

There is growing evidence that some areas in central Europe were, like northern Germany, more resistant to the agricultural crises of the fourteenth and fifteenth centuries than was Germany as a whole. In Poland and portions of Russia, it appears that population growth continued during the course of the late fourteenth century and that there was substantial economic progress in this area. The interpretation of this regional economic development is complex, since it occurred against a background of earlier political and economic disaster. Consequently, it may be viewed, at least in some aspects, as partial recovery rather than as sustained growth. In Russia, the effects of the Mongol invasions of the thirteenth century—economic and demographic catastrophe—reduced the economy to low levels and anticipated by a hundred years the disasters of the west. The period of recovery and reconstruction in the late fourteenth century may easily look like growth when contrasted with western Europe in decline, but we know too little at present to be able to distinguish accurately that portion of the growth which was genuinely new from that that was simply rebuilding. Population did increase, and in the wake of this expansion, arable lands were extended; in a portion of northeastern Russia something of a colonization movement even developed. The level of monetary sophistication may also have risen in some areas of Poland and Russia during the late fourteenth and early fifteenth centuries, as western money flowed into the vast hinterlands of central Europe in search of furs. The increasing availability of money may, if only to a limited degree, have boosted some peasants to a higher level of independence by encouraging the commutation of labor services to money payments. On the other hand, the great wealth of the central European plains lay in agriculture, more particularly in the cultivation of grain. It was not until the general European population rise of the late fifteenth century, which again made food scarce and land dear, that the international market for central European grain really developed. When it did, it was the peasants who suffered, as the lords succeeded in imposing a new serfdom upon them in response to the new profitability of agricultural exports in a rising market.

Indeed, in the lands of central Europe east of the Elbe, the rigor with which the nobility suppressed the peasants renders judgments about peasant welfare somewhat simpler than they are for the west. In the west, labor laws were imposed by the state, hated by the peasants, and almost universally evaded. In the east, the position of the state was weaker, and it was further eroded during the course of the fourteenth-century crises. As a result, the power of the nobility grew to fill the vacuum, and in many regions, brutal repression of the peasantry ensued. Faced by economic crisis in the fourteenth century, the nobles used their political power to obtain forced labor; confronted with the more pleasing prospects of high profits from the rising grain exports of the late fifteenth century, the nobles used their political power to introduce the so-called "second serfdom." The sixteenth-century enclosure movement in England was a response to similar opportunities for profit in the west, but it did not entail the loss of personal freedom for the peasant that resulted in eastern Europe, where, in Prussia, for example, a fugitive from the land could be hanged on the spot quite legally and without any pretense of a trial. Whatever gains the eastern European peasantry may have enjoyed in the immediate train of the economic and political dislocations of the mid-fourteenth century, they were very quickly lost over the course of the next hundred years.

Spain

Our discussion of agriculture has been confined, thus far, within the broad boundaries of the great European plain, where grain was the principal product, where the three-field system was common, and where the substitutes for grain production were limited by the climate. In the south, along the shores of the Mediterranean, agriculture was more varied; the problems entailed by the population decline of the fourteenth century were different in nature, and consequently, more diversity is evident in the regional responses and solutions designed to overcome them. Despite differences in crops and climate, however, the rural economy of the south was closely interconnected with that of the north.

In Spain, from the early Middle Ages, agriculture had struck a delicate balance between cereal cultivation and sheep raising. After the introduction of the North African Merino sheep, probably during the mid-thirteenth century, but not generalized until late in the century, the balance began to shift; herding assumed a more and more important role in Spanish agriculture. Sheep moved across Spain, following the grass and the rainfall, wintering in the warm south and traveling north as the Mediterranean summer brought drought to the southern regions. The paths, or *cañadas*, along which the sheep migrated were never clearly defined; intrusions, either by the flocks into cultivated fields or by farmers extending their arable land into the sheepwalks, were both common and violently condemned by the injured parties. From the farmer's point of view, the only factor compensating him for the passage of the sheep was the possibility of collecting, either on, or for, his fields, the manure left by the passing herds. At worst, the herds might destroy the crops along their route. The herdsman, in his turn, viewed each farm as an encroachment on the natural pasture. Under these circumstances, it is no wonder that considerable hostility developed between farmers and herdsmen. It was ultimately the farmer who lost in the ensuing power struggle. In 1273, King Alfonso of Castile founded a vast guild incorporating all the sheep herders in his kingdom, and granted to this guild, or Mesta, extensive privileges, detrimental to the farming population. Grants of privilege increased in proportion to the financial needs of the Crown, since the Mesta paid subsidies in return for royal support. Pastures were extended at the expense of arable, especially during the fifteenth century, and the interests of the cereal growers were systematically neglected. Payments to the Crown by the Mesta, each justifying and requiring an extension of privilege, became a major source of royal revenue. Agriculture was, by nature, less centralized, both geographically and structurally, and hence it was harder to tax. As grain prices fell during the later Middle Ages, it became progressively poorer and therefore less interesting to a revenue-hungry crown. Ultimately, the privileges granted to the Mesta accelerated the decline of agriculture and further lowered its value in the eyes of the Castilian monarchy, which was constantly pressed for cash.

As the price of wool was at once more stable and more resistant to the economic problems of the fourteenth and fifteenth centuries than were grain prices, the policy of supporting sheep raising at the expense of cereal cultivation made sense economically as well as fiscally. On the other hand, the market for wool was not unlimited. Spanish wool found two principal outlets; the textile industry of Flanders and the Low Countries was by far the more important, but considerable trade was also established with Italy. From 1300 on, the Spanish contribution to international wool supplies grew, eventually causing profound dislocations in the traditional wool markets. The English had long supplied raw wool for the textile industry of the Low Countries, but after the middle of the fourteenth century, England began to develop a cloth industry of her own. We may recall here the growth of English rural textile manufacturing during the late fourtenth and early fifteenth centuries, when some landholders, finding themselves squeezed by falling agricultural profits, endeavored to recoup their losses through industrial undertakings. Partly as a result of English competition in cloth making and partly because of political and economic difficulties indigenous to the continent, the Flemish textile industry fell upon hard times in the late fourteenth century, and the output of cloth dropped sharply. Between 1310 and 1390, for example, the number of finished cloths produced at Ypres declined from 90,000 per year to less than 20,000. Under these circumstances, Spanish wool exports must have been supplanting wool from other sources, rather than providing new supplies to supplement existing sources, as would have been the case in a growing industry. It does not seem unlikely, therefore, that the rapid decline of English wool exports was attributable, at least in part, to increased Spanish competition. From levels as high as 45,000 sacks per year in the early fourteenth century, English exports declined to an average of less than 10,000 sacks during most of the fifteenth century and even dropped below 5,000 sacks during the bleak fourteen-thirties. Despite Spain's probable success in displacing English wool from the northern markets, the falling level of cloth production at Ypres and the older textile centers of Flanders, coinciding as it did with the wholesale conversion of arable to pasture throughout northwestern Europe and hence with increasing local supplies of wool, must have limited greatly the size of the market open to Spanish wool in the north. In the south also, Spanish wool may have partially supplanted the English product during the course of the fifteenth century. Castilian wool from the Merino sheep was of the highest quality, and while not a perfect substitute for English wool, it was of prime importance in the manufacture of the high-quality cloth that increasingly became a specialty of Italy, particularly of Florence, during the late fourteenth century. Florence produced less woolen cloth, both in quantity and in absolute value, at the end than at the beginning of the century, but each cloth was twice as costly, as the Florentines sought to exploit the still active market for extravagant luxury. Spain's geographical position, located as she was on the major sea route from Italy to England, gave her the opportunity to interpose her wool and to satisfy much of the Italian demand for fine short staple wool before Italian traders reached England. The consequences were serious for England; as Italians found less and less need to purchase English wool, the English export market progressively weakened, and the Italians found fewer and fewer goods, other than money, to take back from their trading expeditions to the north. The Spanish, recognizing its value, carefully guarded their monopoly of the Merino sheep and prohibited the export of breeding stock in 1313, 1315, 1322, and 1339. The monarchy gave every privilege to the sheep raisers incorporated in the Mesta. Geographical location aided the wool industry in Spain, while the Hundred Years' War and Edward III's exploitation of the wool trade for his own financial needs created new obstacles for English wool exports. These circumstances gave Spain a temporary competitive advantage, and it is hardly possible to view the international wool market in the later Middle Ages without concluding that Spain's advances derived, at least in part, from England's losses.

The fourteenth and fifteenth centuries were an age in which the products of specialized agriculture were more favored than the traditional foods. Spain was in a peculiarly fortunate position to benefit from this fact. Her geographical position made her the first

Mediterranean country on the sea route from the north, but more significantly, perhaps, her diverse historical experience became an asset in a time of agricultural crisis. The Arab conquest of Spain in the century following the death of Mohammed had placed the Iberian Peninsula under the domination of a culture more advanced than any extant in western Europe in the eighth century. Consequently, the irrigation systems and agricultural techniques of the Romans were preserved, rebuilt, and complemented by the addition of such Arab innovations as the *norias,* a chain-and-bucket irrigation pump. New crops, fruits, and vegetables such as sugar, cotton, citrus fruit, peaches, strawberries, rice, figs, dates, specialties such as almonds and saffron and finally mulberry trees and silk worms were introduced by the Arabs. With the exception of the region around Granada, the Spanish conquest of the Arab territories was accomplished by the beginning of our period. Consequently, despite some contraction in crops as a result of the displacement of the Moors, the Castilian, and especially the Aragonese, monarchies gained access to a highly developed and specialized agricultural area. The crops grown were ideal for the purpose of adding color, zest, and variety to the bland diets endured by northerners during the later Middle Ages; at the same time, the reduced costs of ordinary foods permitted greater expenditures on products that flattered the senses. An active international market developed in citrus fruits, sugar, saffron, silk, and almonds—all of which sold for high and rising prices during the latter portion of the fourteenth century. Again, Spain was able to derive gain from the losses suffered by the landlords and farmers of the north.

Italy

Italy, like Spain, was a land in which climatic and geographical conditions allowed remarkable agricultural variety; like Spain, also, Italy had benefited over the centuries from contact with Arab farming, science, and culture. Together, these two factors go far toward providing an explanation for the diversity of views among modern historians concerning the prosperity—or lack of it—in Italian agriculture during the fourteenth and fifteenth centuries. The agrarian society was too complex to permit a simple answer to the question of prosperity *versus* decline; in Italy, defined as the modern geographical nation including Sicily, incredible poverty marched alongside legendary affluence. One distinction, however—perhaps the clearest that can be made—is that between the agriculture of the south and that of the north. In the Sicilian south (that is, southern Italy and the island of Sicily), the rural economy had traditionally provided large grain exports in spite of its relatively backward technology, which had remained basically unchanged since Roman times. Active world markets, the flourishing cities of northern Italy, and, as the pressures on food supplies grew during the thirteenth and fourteenth centuries, even southern France were eager to purchase the Sicilian grain surpluses. During the fourteenth century, these distant markets began to evaporate; famine in the first fifty years and plague in the second fifty had substantially reduced the European population, simultaneously lowering the aggregate demand for grain and increasing the possibility that local sources could satisfy demands formerly met only through imports. Grain prices everywhere fell during the later Middle Ages, driving northern landlords and farmers to seek new markets as well as new crops. With surpluses available, the search for new markets caused German grain at low prices to flow into northern Italy in competition with the grain of Sicily. Furthermore, after the late thirteenth century, the widespread use of large, round ships at once gave the northern cities the advantages of reduced shipping costs for grain and easier access to distant sources of inexpensive supplies. The combination of these factors meant agricultural ruin for the grain-growing districts of southern Italy. Arable reverted to waste, villages disappeared, and population fell, not only through the effects of plague and malaria, but also through migration to the cities and even to the north, as migrants sought to fill the population gap left by the plague in that more prosperous region. From the fourteenth century on, southern Italy became an impoverished, backward region peopled by an increasingly wretched peasantry.

Even in the south of Italy, however, despite the over-all agrarian malaise, there were certain crops that bestowed a fraction of prosperity upon a fortunate few in some limited areas. Sugar, almost exclusively a product of the south, enjoyed a lively and rising demand during the late fourteenth and early fifteenth centuries. An exotic product at the time, Arabic both in origin and in name, sugar appealed to northern tastes, expanding as they were in response to the fall in the price of other basic foods. Unfortunately for the Sicilians, their temporary sugar monopoly was not defensible in the long run; competitors swiftly developed, to threaten the Italian markets. Portuguese settlement of the islands off the coast of Africa had begun early in the fifteenth century under the guidance of Henry the Navigator, and by the fourteen-twenties, the Madeiras were being colonized. Within thirty years, Sicilian sugar had been transplanted to the Portuguese islands and become well enough established to justify the construction of a water mill for the purpose of crushing the cane. The Sicilian monopoly was thereafter broken. Sweet wine, which had been one of the most valuable exports of southern Italy and the Mediterranean islands, suffered the same fate as sugar. During the fifteenth century, the Portuguese transplanted Sicilian vines to the new islands, where once they were established, they became the base for the world-famous Madeira wines which replaced Sicilian growths on the tables of affluent northerners.

Within Italy itself, the gradual northward diffusion of those specialty crops not climatically limited to the south tended to erode the earlier competitive advantages of lower Italy. Fruit and nuts from southern Italy found an actively growing market during the later Middle Ages, but with time, the market was divided by the increasing growth of these products in northern Italy, where urban investors in agriculture sought out such high-value crops that found ready demand at home and abroad. At the same time, Spanish competition in these items heightened. Olive oil was primarily a southern commodity, but butter, a product of the north, was a substitute, albeit an expensive one; in the fifteenth century, butter from Lombardy was making inroads in central Italy as far south as Rome. In dyestuffs also, northern Italy steadily gained at the expense of the southern and central portions of the country; woad from Lombardy dominated the markets of Italy by the fifteenth century and even became an important export to countries farther north.

At this point, it is useful to refer again to events in Spain and in northwestern Europe. The attempts of northerners to replace falling wheat and grain revenues led to more intensive cultivation of dyestuffs; the Cistercian farm at Veulerent, cited above, had already witnessed a substantial increase in the acreage devoted to the cultivation of woad—only one example of a quite general trend. Thus woad, while it remained a profitable export, could never yield the monopoly profits that might have accrued to Italy in the absence of alternative sources of supply. The same, of course, may be said for the citrus crops; their prices were very high and their transport difficult, but internationally, the Italians faced the stiff competition of Spain and hence could not derive excessive profit from the trade without losing the market. During the late fourteenth century, for example, Spanish oranges became a frequent English import, although each shipment was small. Even though much of the carrying trade was in the hands of the Italians, Spain's position along the major north–south sea route gave her agriculture an edge over her competitors in southern Italy. The same may be said of Spain's increasing export of rice to northern markets; while it did not exclude the Italian product, the Spanish trade limited both the market and the profit potentially available to Italian growers.

Deprived, during the fourteenth and fifteenth centuries, of much of the wealth earned in the grain trade, southern Italy directed her resources to the production of the more exotic products of the Mediterranean. The shift from the extensive cultivation of a bulk crop was painful enough; the attempt to replace the lost grain revenues through greater attention to high-value luxury crops such as sugar, wine, dyestuffs, nuts, and fruits was condemned to achieve no more than partial success even under the most favorable circumstances. History and economics, however, combined to frustrate even this slim hope; the Portuguese discoveries destroyed the market for the two most profitable exports, wine and sugar. Spanish competition held down the profits from the remaining crops. From the fourteenth century on, southern Italy slid ever downward.

To the north of Italy during the late fourteenth and early fifteenth centuries, economic conditions seem to have gone against the trend evident elsewhere. Portions of the north display considerable evidence of agrarian development, particularly in the early fifteenth century; townsmen from the still affluent northern cities directed their free funds toward the land. As a result, older systems of tenure and agrarian organization fell, or rather, experienced significant acceleration in a decline evident from at least the twelfth century. Traditional landlords, especially the clerical ones, suffered when confronted with the competition and sharp dealing of the financially sophisticated urban investors. Church rents were often, but not always, more rigidly fixed than their secular counterparts, and consequently clerical landlords were willing to grant long-term leases to speculators in return for small increases in rents. Often these leases became permanent and hence virtually equivalent to total alienation of the Church land. The impact of this practice in some regions was striking. One scholar, Carlo Cipolla, has calculated that by the sixteenth century, the Church held no more than 10 to 15 per cent of the land in the north of Italy, whereas in the south it still controlled several centuries later between 65 and 70 per cent of the land.[7] High labor costs following the plague compounded the Church's difficulties, as did the financing of its expenditures through credit obtained from urban moneylenders on terms that could never be fulfilled.

Rationalization of tenure systems was but one of the factors giving momentum to the development of northern agriculture; it was not accomplished without major dislocations and great suffering among those who were displaced. The use of credit as a weapon for gaining control of productive resources affected the humble as well as the mighty. Far down in the ranks of rural society, peasants who sold crops for forward delivery found themselves ensnared in the moneylenders' nets. Many peasants, overburdened with debt and without hope of ever redeeming their lands from pawn, attempted to migrate to the cities. Here they were greeted by restrictive legislation that supported the coalition of urban, industrial, and agricultural wealth against the interests of the peasants. Advances in freedom—at least statutory freedom—were gained, as they had been since the thirteenth century, only for a price, often a high one, usually inclusion in the urban tax system. Such inclusion, as in France, acted to increase the peasants' need for money and to render them more subject both to speculators who advanced funds in return for ultimate economic domination and to the power of the urban mar-

---

[7] C. M. Cipolla, "Une Crise ignorée: comment s'est perdue la propriété ecclésiastique dans l'Italie du nord entre le xi⁰ et le xvi⁰ siècle," *Annales-Economies, Sociétés, Civilisations,* II (1947), 317–27.

ketplace, which was controlled and regulated by precisely the same coalition of the wealthy that was squeezing the peasants at every other juncture. Growth there was in some portions of the agrarian sector of northern Italy, but it was not an unmixed benefit, as the numerous small farmers who were displaced in the name of progress learned to their sorrow.

What did the growth consist of, and what were its causes? For reasons that will be developed later in more detail, several of the towns of extreme northern Italy experienced an industrial and commercial boom during the late fourteenth and early fifteenth centuries. Milan, in the center of Lombardy, developed a vigorous armament industry, supplying the needs of both sides during the Hundred Years' War. Venice, in her turn, specialized in the provision of luxury goods calculated to console those northerners threatened by the disasters of war, famine, plague, and the recurrent series of catastrophes that stalked Europe during the later Middle Ages.

So long as the industrial and some of the commercial towns of the north remained active, the rural economy could find ready markets for its products. Even the sharp decline in the population of northern cities, most evident in the late fourteenth century, did not destroy regional agricultural markets. Since the towns, in the best of times, were unable to find adequate food in the surrounding countryside, they had become accustomed to consuming the entire regional grain output without, in all likelihood meeting half their needs. When population, world grain prices, and even shipping costs fell, the towns could benefit from cheaper imports, but shipping costs did not fall enough to allow the northern urban communities to dispense with local food sources. River transport within the rich Po Valley was inevitably less expensive than ocean transport costs from Sicily or the grain-growing regions of Germany plus the cost of local distribution.

With markets assured and competition at least partially excluded by transport costs, particularly in the inland towns, the agrarian economy in some regions of northern Italy flourished. Money from the still affluent cities was available for investment in land; the cities in turn provided markets for the products of the soil. Finally, land rationalization may have contributed to an increase in the efficiency and hence in the productivity of the land. Canals as well as drainage and irrigation systems were improved and extended during the fifteenth century to exploit the fertile Po Valley. Large estates were assembled by merchants and run on the same principles of cost-consciousness and rational accounting that were prevalent in large-scale, urban business. This in turn meant that agriculture in northern Italy became highly market-sensitive, concentrating on those products which found ready sale.

As we have already observed, in the fourteenth and fifteenth centuries such products very often were primary or secondary luxury products or industrial raw materials. Grain, of course, for reasons peculiar to northern Italy's industrial and commercial position at this time, derived secondary status as an industrial and commercial good from proximity to cities engaged in trade. Other crops also benefited. During the later Middle Ages, mulberry trees were introduced to the north, and the cultivation of silkworms filled a portion, probably still a small portion, of the regional, industrial demand for this most expensive and highly sought-after product. Dyestuffs, primarily woad, became an increasingly prevalent northern crop that found international markets in the world's textile centers as well as domestic markets in northern Italy. Hemp and flax—again, crops that met industrial requirements—were northern crops whose demand was not so sharply reduced by population decline as was the demand for wheat throughout most areas of northwestern Europe. Sheep raising also expanded, but especially in the south, in the fourteenth and fifteenth centuries and contributed to the supply of wool for the coarse cloth suitable for the less wealthy citizens of northern Italy. Demand for luxury goods, in those cities still benefiting from commercial and industrial prosperity during the later Middle Ages was strong enough to create substantial markets for the high-quality wines of upper Italy, for saffron, and for the citrus fruit that began to be developed in that region from the end of the thirteenth century. Citrus fruit and some of the best vintages of wine were products that did not travel well; their cultivation was aided by proximity to such major markets as Milan and Venice.

Indeed, this latter fact is at once the secret of northern Italian agricultural prosperity during the fourteenth and fifteenth centuries and a cause for caution before one generalizes from this small region to the whole of Europe. A small fragment of the surface of northern Italy prospered while the greater portion suffered. Perhaps the single most important factor responsible for the regional prosperity was the very inadequacy of the agrarian economy of northern Italy in relation to the urban economy. Since the countryside there had not been able to feed the cities since the twelfth century at least, its agriculture never really suffered the effects of the demographic decline so fatal for agriculture elsewhere. It was the close relationship between the populous cities and the limited countryside that encouraged investment in the land in northern Italy, in the immediate environs of some French cities, and even in certain regions of Germany. But only in northern Italy were the urban centers both large enough and active enough to exhaust quickly and completely local supplies of produce; only there was there sufficient variety of climate and of industrial and commercial activity to allow the broad diversification of crops that created agricultural wealth in a period of general decline. Even there, however, the wealth created was absorbed and engrossed by the moneylenders and landlords resident in the cities; the peasant received little of the profit. Towns produced rural wealth by investing in the land and by consuming the products of the soil; towns harvested the wealth by collecting the taxes, the rents, and the incomes from their investments. It is to the urban economy that we must now turn.

3

Town and Industry

POPULATION

Reduced to its basic elements, a town is nothing more than a mass of people dwelling within narrow geographical confines. Despite its apparent simplicity, this definition stresses the essential features of urban life and reveals the roots of many urban economic, social, and political problems and policies. How may the people be fed, housed, and ordered when the area is small and the people are many? Can they be taxed by the government, or do their numbers render the townspeople politically dangerous? Should the city government control the surrounding countryside in order to protect the town's supplies of food and raw material? Should it regulate immigration, the organization of industry, and the labor force? To what extent does the very size of the town compel the urban government to intrude in the personal lives and economic affairs of the citizens? Before attempting to discuss these and similar questions, it is necessary to have a firm impression, at least in outline, of the demographic history of Europe's urban centers.

Medieval towns were on the whole quite small; a few, mainly in Italy, such as Milan, Naples, Venice, and Florence, attained population levels of about 100,000 prior to the Black Death; some eastern cities, such as Constantinople, may have had double that figure. For a time, Paris was considered to have been one of the largest cities in medieval Europe, but recent research has reduced the estimated population from an unrealistic 240,000 to a more credible level of 80,000. It was a rare city in northern Europe that exceeded 50,000 inhabitants. London was probably slightly below that figure;

with the exception of Ghent, which may have boasted 50,000 or 60,000 inhabitants, the great cloth towns of Flanders were much smaller. In Germany, Cologne was the largest town, but during our period, its population seems to have been well below the 50,000 mark; the remaining German towns do not appear to have grown much above half that figure. Farther north, in Scandinavia, urban populations remained low, and one does not find even such a modest population center as London.

Towns, then, were small, but their relative importance should not be measured by size alone. Since they were the repositories of much of the technical skill in industry, trade, and finance and further, since they had considerable economic impact, both as consumers of agricultural goods and as suppliers of manufactures to the rural hinterlands, their leverage in the medieval economy was very great. The economic vicissitudes of the towns were swiftly transmitted to the rest of the countryside. As a result, given the limitations of medieval statistics, it is perhaps more revealing and more judicious as well, to consider the demographic history of towns as a dynamic rather than as a static element in the economy and to concentrate upon the rate and direction of change rather than upon absolute levels of population. We have already presented some statistics on the rate of expansion of town walls that suggest that an expansion of urban populations during the period 1100–1350 was followed by contraction, or at least by stagnation, in the subsequent century. We will now consider more direct evidence, drawn from diverse regions on a comparative basis. First, however, another word of caution is required. Medieval population figures normally emanate from records at one remove from actual head counts or census material; in order to generate estimates of total population, tax rolls, hearth counts, military service lists, and the like must be converted through the application of some arbitrary multiplier representative of family size. Needless to say, the selection of the precise multiplier is a very delicate process. Without additional information, how can we know, for example, whether a medieval hearth represents three, four, five, or even six persons? Since the needed information is rarely forthcoming, we are left with a difficult problem but one which, under favorable circumstances, may be circumvented. Because our concern here is primarily with rates of change, we are on fairly solid ground if we can assume that shifts in the number of hearths accurately measure shifts in the general population; but even here, circumspection is required. The hearths enumerated on a list may be nothing more than abstract tax units representing the fiscal obligation of an entire city, but without direct reference to its population; such tax units would measure economic as well as demographic changes. The same may be said of direct tax registers; if only those citizens with more than some minimum level of wealth or income were liable to taxation, then demographic inferences drawn from the tax rolls over time will be biased by economic change. We might mistake a period of affluence for a period of rapid population growth. Conversely, if the government required more money, it is possible that the number of hearths recorded might increase simply in reflection of the government's endeavor to extract additional sums from a stable population.

Despite the uncertainty involved in evaluating the demographic statistics from any single town considered individually, there is strength in mutual corroboration. If many sets of dubious statistics, independently gathered from many different regions and by different processes, all point in the same direction, it seems reasonable to accept that direction as the general trend, even if the absolute statistical measures remain in doubt. Thus, the following graph presents evidence from a number of towns simultaneously. The scale is cast in percentage terms in order to facilitate comparisons among the various towns and to illuminate trends rather than absolute levels of urban population.

Unfortunately, as is apparent from the graph, there are few urban series that enable us to trace the demographic history of towns very far back into the thirteenth century. The figures for Florence and Siena, however, do extend into that period and confirm our earlier impression, based on town walls, of a rapid growth in the numbers of urban dwellers during the high Middle Ages. Further, the credibility of the individual figures is enhanced by the close parallel between the over-all patterns of the two cities; additional support may be derived from the similarity between the Italian urban figures and the general population curve of England (Graph II, p. 28). It would appear that the city curves reflect and perhaps ac-

GRAPH IV Population of Nineteen Towns (Expressed as a Percentage of the Population Peak)

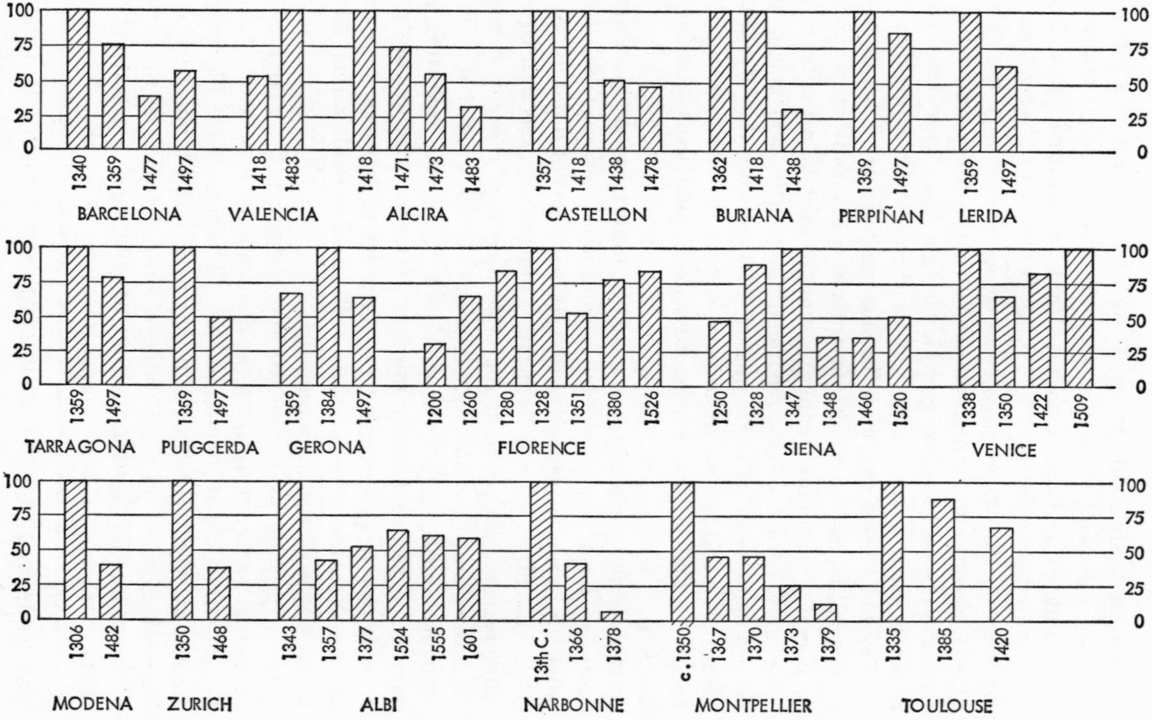

LERIDA — 1497, 1359

PERPIÑAN — 1497, 1359

BURIANA — 1438, 1418, 1362

CASTELLON — 1478, 1438, 1418, 1357

ALCIRA — 1483, 1473, 1471, 1418

VALENCIA — 1483, 1418

BARCELONA — 1497, 1477, 1359, 1340

VENICE — 1509, 1422, 1350, 1338

SIENA — 1520, 1460, 1348, 1347, 1328, 1250

FLORENCE — 1526, 1380, 1351, 1328, 1280, 1260, 1200

GERONA — 1497, 1384, 1359

PUIGCERDA — 1497, 1359

TARRAGONA — 1497, 1359

TOULOUSE — 1420, 1385, 1335

MONTPELLIER — 1379, 1373, 1370, 1367, c.1350

NARBONNE — 1378, 1366, 13th C.

ALBI — 1601, 1555, 1524, 1377, 1357, 1343

ZURICH — 1468, 1350

MODENA — 1482, 1306

centuate the general demographic patterns of western Europe, particularly during the period before the Black Death. We have already observed that the rapid growth of population severely strained the agricultural sector in the late thirteenth and early fourteenth centuries; let us now investigate the economic consequences of that demographic expansion in the cities.

PROVISIONMENT

The rapid population growth prior to 1350 forced many towns to regulate the regional trade by which they survived. The problems associated with the provisioning of large numbers of people, isolated or semi-isolated from the soil, increasingly drew the attention of the urban governments. As population grew and the agricultural supply areas perforce expanded, the possibility that a few rich monopolists or even the rural population itself might gain a stranglehold over the cities became very real indeed. From the thirteenth century on, urban governments expressed their recognition and fear of this possibility through an increasing proliferation of ordinances designed to defend the food supplies and to assure the regular flow of agricultural goods into the cities. Some of these ordinances endeavored to maintain free trade in grain and to prevent monopoly. Laws forbidding forestalling, engrossing, and regrating—broadly, the purchase of commodities outside the confines of the urban market for later resale at a profit—proliferated throughout the towns of Europe. Special supervised markets were

GRAPH IV

SOURCES: J. Vicens Vives, *Historia Social y Económica de España y America,* Vol. II, Barcelona, 1957, for Barcelona, Valencia, Alcira, Castellon, Buriana, Perpiñan, Lerida, Tarragona, Puigcerda and Gerona; Alfred Doren, *Storia económica dell'-Italia nel medio evo,* trans. G. Luzzatto, Padova, 1937, for Florence, Siena, Venice, and Modena; R. S. Lopez, "Hard Times and Investment in Culture," *The Renaissance, Medieval or Modern,* D. C. Heath & Co., Boston, 1959, for Zurich; G. Prat, "Albi et la peste noire," *Annales du Midi,* 1952, for Albi to 1357; F. Lot, *Recherches sur la population et la superficie des cités remontrant à la période Gallo-Romaine,* Vol. II, Paris, 1950, for Albi from 1377; G. Fagniez, *Documents relatif à l'histoire de l'industrie et du commerce en France,* Vol. II, Paris 1900, for Narbonne and Montpellier.

established in many cities, such as Gracechurch, Queenhithe, Newgate, and Billingsgate in London or the Halles, the Grève, and the Rue de la Juiverie in Paris. Their purpose was to prevent speculation and the withholding of grain or other food for extortionate prices. Neither in London nor in Paris could food, once it had been presented in the specified markets, be removed from them for more profitable sale elsewhere. Such regulations were clearly designed to insure the survival of open competition unhampered by monopolistic practices; grain prices were usually allowed to find their own level, while the municipal authorities acted to prevent abuses of the market power held by food suppliers over the cities. Experiments in national price control of grain were sometimes made— one may cite attempts by Philip IV of France in 1305 or by Edward II of England during the great famine of 1315–17—but these failed disastrously and were quickly abandoned when grain disappeared from the markets.

Other types of food control were more direct and restrictive. At the first level, efforts were made to avert famine through the regulation of grain exports, particularly during periods of crisis. Equally evident in this category were attempts to divert, by means of direct legislation, the normal routes of grain transport so as to favor a particular region or city. In France in 1375, for example, the Duke of Anjou authorized the officials of the town of Toulouse to seize grain as it passed through the area around the city; the order was countermanded within the year by Charles V and the freedom of grain shipments in southern France was restored. Practically all towns, regions, and countries forbade the export of grain during famine periods. Sometimes the prohibitions occurred at a national level; England had to negotiate on a national level with France for the right to purchase grain during the famine of 1315–17, since the French king was the only authority who could allow exports during that disastrous period. Local and regional controls, however, were more usual and in general more suited to the problems of medieval food supply and transportation. Local crises occurred regularly and could only be met with delay and difficulty if it became necessary to resort to imports; delay, of course, in the provision of food could mean death for substantial numbers. Italian towns had recognized this early and sought to control the surrounding countryside. By the thirteenth century, Venice claimed economic hegemony over the accessible reaches of the Po Valley and also over much of the immediate southern hinterland. In addition, Venice used her political power over her colony at Ragusa, on the Dalmatian coast, to compel the Ragusans to carry grain, but nothing else, to Venice. In this case, the provisionment policy had developed far beyond internal regulation of marketing and consumption; it was instead an endeavor to establish monopsonistic control over a very extensive geographical region. Many Italian cities formulated provisionment policies in order to obtain direct control over the neighboring areas of agricultural production. A significant aspect of urban policy during the twelfth and thirteenth centuries had been the calculated reduction of the political power of nobles and rural landlords through the substitution of urban for feudal authority. Peasants, freed from feudal obligations, became dependent upon the towns and subject to their control; nobles, their feudal dominance reduced, were encouraged to join the urban community, where so long as they were no longer politically dangerous, they could be supported by urban authority and their status exploited as a device for implementing the towns' provisionment policies.

Towns everywhere, despite all efforts to guarantee food supplies and to control the agricultural districts surrounding them, led a precarious existence. It remained necessary to keep close watch over the factors affecting internal food consumption. Thus, many towns sought to control levels of immigration or, at the least, to be conscious of variations in the number of inhabitants so that arrangements could be made for their nutrition. In Italy, special municipal officers were placed in charge of estimating the food requirements in advance, and they were provided with funds for the purchase of enough imported grain to cover the difference between domestic production and the predicted requirements. In northern cities, also, public and private granaries existed to mitigate the ever-present danger of famine. Northern towns developed quite elaborate market regulations, and numerous official posts were created to smooth the concourse between the peasants and the bourgeoisie, but the Italian cities obtained more effective direct control over the countryside and its agricultural production than did the towns of the north. Some exceptions existed in Flanders, but monopsony was more pronounced in the south. In the north, urban food policy was more effective in freeing trade and in preventing monopoly than in obtaining political control over regional food production.

What level of success did medieval provisionment policies attain? The very survival and growth of the towns commend the achievement of urban food policies, since without adequate food flows, the urban communities would simply have withered away. On the other hand, when failures came, they came on a grand scale; municipal policy in Flanders during the great famine of 1315–17 was impotent to overcome the Pan-European grain crisis. The death of 10 per cent of the citizens of Ypres was the price of failure in that town. In London, however, it would appear that, at least among the affluent—those rich enough to leave property by testament—the famine made very little impact; there was no increase in the average number of wills probated during the years of the famine. The experiences of Ypres and London are not statistically comparable, since in the former, all citizens, and in the latter, only the rich citizens, are recorded, but the low London mortality among the affluent is in striking contrast to the rural experience. In the English countryside, the death rate marched upward parallel with the price of grain; private urban stocks and foreign imports had rendered London's upper classes virtually immune from famine in a time when the farmers themselves suffered and died of starvation.

The leaders of medieval towns had been rightly directing considerable emphasis to provisioning problems. Except in extreme circumstances, such policies were successful in assuring adequate subsistence to the upper social levels at all times and to the great majority most of the time during the early fourteenth century. After the mid-century mark, the problems associated with the food supply were notably eased. After that point, we are viewing the reverse side of the agricultural crisis discussed in the preceding chapter. Municipal policy had been able to provide, at least partially, against famine; it proved totally useless before the grim visage of plague. Crowded and unsanitary urban conditions and, as the continuous strain on agrarian productivity began to tell during the early fourteenth century, chronically poor levels of nutrition increased the vulnerability of the towns to contagious disease. The sharp break in the population figures in Graph IV gives some measure of the impact of the plague upon the urban population. Death rates of from 25 to 50 per cent of the total number of inhabitants were not uncommon. In German towns, the mortality was sometimes even greater, ranging from 50 per cent at Magdeburg to between 50 and 70 per cent of the inhabitants of Hamburg and Bremen, according to the estimates of the German historian Reincke. As we have seen, the general decline in population reduced the number of mouths to be fed by more than it reduced the number, or at least the output, of the food producers. Grain prices fell, and towns that had diminished in size no longer had to exercise such great caution in their provisionment policies. After 1350, they could obtain more grain at less cost and with less fear of imminent famine, although famine years still occurred. The population decline was, in some senses, truly a boon for the survivors in the towns, since they were freed from the spectre of starvation; the remaining citizens could expand their diets and enjoy more variety in the food they consumed as long as their incomes remained relatively close to the older levels.

THE STRUCTURE OF INDUSTRY

Urban incomes depended mainly upon industrial and commercial activity, although substantial revenues from other sources did exist. Landholders, resident in the cities, collected their rents from the agricultural hinterland; churchmen drew funds from a wider region than the city alone; officials at various levels of government, from the royal to the municipal, earned their keep without becoming involved, except by choice, in commerce. Finally, there were those who maintained themselves by providing services for others as servants, porters, carters, builders, carpenters, and the like. The latter group was on the fringe of the primary industrial and commercial activities of the town, but their incomes depended on those activities. The former groups—landlords, churchmen, and officials—could perhaps have existed independently of urban commercial activity, but only at the primitive social and cultural levels evident during the early Middle Ages, when cities survived solely because of their role as administrative units.

Commercial and industrial activity was crucial to the survival, growth, and development of the cities of the fourteenth and fifteenth centuries; without manufacturing and trade, the towns would quickly have reverted to the level of the villages of the seventh century, minute and skeletal shadows of urban communities. Let us, then, consider the urban occupations and industrial enterprises in some detail; first, however, it is useful to make some general remarks concerning the nature and structure of industry as a whole during the later Middle Ages. Perhaps the most striking aspect of medieval industry is the miniscule size of each enterprise and the absence—though with a few exceptions—of large-scale fixed capital investment. A master worker with one or two apprentices comprised the typical establishment. Even those enterprises that required far larger supplies of labor did not employ the labor force in concentration, but instead divided the manufacturing process into smaller and smaller stages. There was no firm that vertically represented the cloth industry, for example, with involvement in all stages of production. On the contrary, the industry normally was divided, with spinners separated from weavers, weavers from fullers, fullers from finishers, and the latter from the ultimate wholesale and retail merchants. Even where considerable geographical concentration occurred, as in the case of the Venetian arsenal, the workers were organized on a piecework basis rather than as a single, unified enterprise under one leadership endowed with the power to regulate all phases of manufacture.

Capital equipment in medieval industry consisted mainly of simple tools closely keyed to the man who used them; the skill of the individual artisan was of the utmost importance in the production process. These facts are crucial for understanding the impact of the vast late-fourteenth century population decline upon industry and the urban economy. In agriculture, the reduction of the rural population allowed the survivors to redistribute the land, to acquire larger holdings, and to abandon land that was not fully productive. For this reason, it is highly probable that the average productivity of agricultural workers rose substantially; the collective-inheritance

effect gave each rural worker a larger and more fertile endowment
of land whether he owned it or simply worked on it for others. In
the towns, on the contrary, the inheritance effects on average productivity were far less noticeable. Where there was a one-to-one relationship between the worker and his tools, little additional benefit was gained from access to the capital goods left by victims of the
plague. A farmer with twice as many acres as he held before the
plague might be much, though probably not twice as much, more
productive, but a carpenter with two hammers, or a shoemaker with
two benches, gained little. Indeed, since the skill factor was crucial
in medieval industry, it is very likely that the average productivity
of artisans fell in the immediate wake of each successive visitation
of plague or famine. The rapid increase in the death rate during
such periods may well have outstripped the ability of society, hampered as it was by long terms of apprenticeship and limitations upon
the number of apprentices, to train adequate replacements at the
old levels of skill. During the slow process by which new entrants
achieved technical competence in industry and manufacture, their
contributions to the productive effort must have been less than
those of experienced masters. Unlike the rural economy, the urban
economy could not normally benefit from the greater per capita
quantity of capital; technological factors prevented this, while the
rapid attrition rates within the skilled labor force, resultant upon
the high mortality levels of the fourteenth century, lowered still
further the average level of productivity.

As in the case of all generalizations, some qualifications are necessary. Even in the Middle Ages, some industries were capital-in-
tensive and consequently capable of reaping gains from the inheritance effects of the plague. The fulling process in the woolen
industry—that is, the shrinking and felting of woven cloth—required major investment in fulling mills. The mills, in turn, since
they had to be located on moderately swift and regular water
courses, necessitated investment not only in money, but also in the
commitment of choice sites that had alternative uses. Thus there
was an opportunity cost in placing a fulling mill, rather than a
grain mill, at a select spot on a water course. It is possible, therefore, that the fall in the demand for grain freed certain water
courses for use as fulling mill locations. The success of Sir John

Fastolf at Castle Combe in utilizing the water power on his estates indicates that in this one case, at least, the inheritance effects of plague, by reducing the demand for grain and consequently for scarce water power, worked to the benefit of the textile industry. It is equally possible that the location of fulling mills on the most favorable sites contributed to an increase in the average productivity of the fullers. In the salt trade also, technology may have favored increased productivity among the survivors of the plague. Since most salt was manufactured by evaporation of sea water in shallow pits along the coast, flat land close to the sea in places where the weather was normally fine and warm were at a premium. To the extent that the industry was able to abandon marginal locations and to concentrate in the most suitable sites, average productivity among the salt workers may have risen. In leather making, two factors may have worked in the same direction. The tanning process involved a substantial investment in an inventory of hides for the span of six months to two years during which the leather was soaked in a solution of oak bark and water. The fall in hide prices consequent upon the increased consumption of meat as consumers converted the gains obtained from falling bread prices into more protein-rich diets would have served to reduce the costs of carrying an inventory of hides through the tanning period. Since one man could handle large numbers of hides if he had the capital to buy them, it is again possible that average productivity in the leather industry rose as inventory costs fell.

Fulling, salt, leather—we might include some aspects of metallurgy and smelting in which reduced demands for building timber and the reversion of arable land to forest, as in Germany, may have increased fuel supplies—and a few other industries may have achieved gains in productivity, but we cannot be certain. The economic possibility was there, but without figures revealing total output and total employment in these industries, estimates of labor productivity remain no more than speculation. No weight of analysis, therefore, will be placed upon possible growth in productivity in these industries, but instead, the realization that gains may have occurred will be used to temper an analysis founded upon the absence of increases in productivity in the much wider group of industrial activities where the worker and his tools were so closely interrelated on a one-to-one basis as to preclude any inference of advantage from the inheritance effects of the plague.

In this group of industries, the first effect of higher mortality rates was to reduce sharply the number of artisans without increasing the productivity of those that remained. In some cases, levels of skill certainly fell. Medieval documentation provides few opportunities to evaluate comparative skill levels over time, but in the case of the scribes, the evidence has survived. Rolls of wills preserved in London illuminate two aspects of rapid demographic change; first, the accelerated speed with which scribal hands replace one another in the manuscripts after the middle of the fourteenth century testifies to heightened turnover as successive scribes succumbed to the plague. Second, the increasing irregularity and progressive disintegration of the script itself suggests that the replacements were less and less well trained. In this case, at least, the higher mortality lowered the level of skill to a demonstrable degree; it does not seem unreasonable to assume that the phenomenon was more general and that the difficulty of finding adequately trained artisans afflicted the entire range of industrial and commercial enterprise. Royal regulations in various regions confirm this view. In Paris in 1351, for example, King Jean le Bon issued a royal ordinance relaxing those guild restrictions that limited the number of apprentices in the shoemakers' craft. In another ordinance, he decreed freedom of contract in apprenticeship and ended the requirement of proof of capacity as a condition of entrance into any trade on a general basis. His son Charles V granted cloth workers who sought safety in Rouen during the Hundred Years' War the right to practice their craft without the formality of apprenticeship. Everywhere, after the first visitation of the plague, ordinances and statutes designed to regulate wages and to eliminate the labor scarcity multiplied; in 1366, Florence went so far as to allow the importation of pagan slaves. Such attempts usually met with little success, since it was an unalterable economic fact that labor, particularly skilled labor, was everywhere in short supply and likely to remain so because of the time required for training. The Paris ordinances cited were obviously intended to shorten the training period, but it is inconceivable that legislation alone could overcome the need for acquiring the skills of the craft.

Considerations of productivity and levels of skill permit us to generalize in regard to industry as a whole. We are viewing, in fact, the basic element that permeated all industry and that placed constraints upon the levels of attainable production in the manufacturing sector. The supply of manufactures was rigidly tied to the number of workers and to their technological prowess. Hence, in contrast to the situation in agriculture, overproduction was not an immediate problem in industry. The presence of more capital per worker did not foster significant gains in output; the difficulty of training, or of finding, skilled artisans tended, if anything, to reduce productivity. At the same time, the increased desire for luxury diverted those with the greatest skills from more common tasks. With stable or reduced productivity and fewer workers, there was little chance of excess production. Thus, for a time, the towns enjoyed a favored economic position, insulated against the problems evident in agriculture.

MARKETS

What, however, of the other side of the coin? What factors affected the market for manufactured goods? In dealing with this question, we may start with the initial presumption that the demand for manufactured goods of all classes was more elastic than that for the basic food grains. As declining grain prices freed money for other types of consumption, the per capita urban demand for manufactured goods grew. This pattern is identical to the shift in demand that led to greater per capita expenditures on meat, wine, butter, and certain spices; free funds sought new outlets in those commodities that did not satiate the appetite so readily as bread. Within the ample range of manufactured goods, many products fitted this category.

The sharp rise in mortality rates during the later Middle Ages diverted money from the bread grains into luxury foods and manufactured items, but this was not its only impact. There is an increasing body of evidence to show that individual preference patterns, both in consumption and in investment, were affected as well. Life was short and, to the medieval man who had endured plague, famine, malaria, and war, must have seemed to be growing shorter. The overriding presence of death appears to have had profound influence upon the demand for goods. Many men reasoned that what was not consumed today would be consumed by their heirs tomorrow; consequently, many turned to a life of worldly gratification. There was good reason for this view. Increased mortality, even discounting the desire to live for the moment, produced an immediate effect upon consumption patterns as many citizens inherited wealth from deceased relatives, while others simply helped themselves and scavenged the goods of the dead, whether related or not. The initial result of the series of plagues in the second half of the fourteenth century was a dramatic increase in the per capita wealth of the survivors; money, gold and silver plate, and durable goods of all sorts remained to be divided among perhaps one-third fewer people than before the plague. In the French town of Albi, the proportion of citizens with fortunes greater than one hundred livres doubled between 1343 and 1357; in the same period the percentage with less than ten livres dropped by half. At every social level, per capita wealth rose. In London, the enormous increase in the number of wills subjected to probate during the thirteen-fifties and -sixties reflects a similar concentration of wealth in the hands of the survivors, and there is no reason to suppose that experience differed in other cities of western Europe. In the south in 1351 Matteo Villani, describing Florence, put the case succinctly:

> No sooner had the plague ceased than . . . since men were few and since by hereditary succession they abounded in earthly goods, they forgot the past as though it had never been and gave themselves up to a more shameful and disordered life than they had led before . . . and the common people by reason of the abundance and superfluity that they found would no longer work at their accustomed trades; they wanted the dearest and most delicate foods . . . while children and common women clad themselves in all the fair and costly garments of the illustrious who had died.[1]

Boccaccio's reference, in his introduction to the *Decameron*, to those who "thought the sure cure for the plague was to drink and

---

[1] Quoted in Millard Meiss, *Painting in Florence and Siena after the Black Death* (New York: Harper & Row, Publishers, 1964), p. 67.

be merry, to go about singing and amusing themselves, satisfying every appetite they could" and who "spent day and night going from tavern to tavern drinking immoderately" and "doing only those things which pleased them" provides additional literary evidence of the mutation of consumption patterns. Under the stress of plague, consumption had become for some an urgent matter. Wealth, or more accurately, the painful process of postponing pleasure while conserving or accumulating wealth, became for many an irrelevant act. Display, ornamentation, and the gratification of every personal desire seemed valid goals, doubly justified by increased funds and the nearness of death. Not all behaved in this fashion, of course, and even among those suddenly rich who did, reckless consumption could not last forever.

Substantial investment did occur, for example, in the agricultural regions of northern Italy, in the countryside surrounding French cities, and in the English textile industry, indicating that some entrepreneurs were paying more obeisance to the long future than to the immediate moment. But this was a phenomenon that attained its peak in the fifteenth century, well after the first shock of the plague had been absorbed.

Still others turned their attention entirely away from the things of this mortal world and sought to win grace in the next. If life was short, it was well to be warned and to prepare for judgment; the only sound investment in so troubled a world was in the well-being of the soul. As a result of the plague, investments in spiritual grace rose in three ways. First, the increase in the death rate automatically swelled the numbers of legacies to the Church, since it was customary to include provisions for the Church and charity in testaments of the time. Secondly, the elevated death rate, by destroying entire families and leaving many of the wealthy without heirs, encouraged larger individual bequests to the Church at the same time as it increased their number. Thirdly, since the incidence of death had risen so dramatically, many pious citizens endeavored to spend their remaining short span of years in preparation for the eternal life; among this group, increased bequests and gifts to the Church were common. Growing sums found their way into the coffers of the Church.

One effect of the plague, then, at least in the third quarter of the fourteenth century, was to reduce the desire to save and, consequently, to invest. Exceptions existed, of course, but the most striking feature of the period after the Black Death was a vast increase in consumption, particularly luxury consumption. In many countries, government policy may have contributed to this reaction. Growing demands for funds for use in war mobilized money that otherwise might have lain idle. The pressures of war in France and England drew money from the peasants in taxes, from the urban communities in both loans and taxes, and from bankers, both foreign and domestic. In France, during the fourteenth century, there were even several ordinances that required the nobles to carry specified portions of their bullion and plate to the mints for coinage into money; so far had fiscal necessity forced the mobilization of idle funds. Under the combined pressures of government finance, psychological reactions to the plague, and the inheritance effects of the resultant mortality, substantial demand for manufactured goods was created. At the same time, the correlative reduction in both the desire for and the possibility of saving limited investment, while the increased mortality rates diminished the number of trained artisans capable of producing the goods that were demanded. Under these circumstances, we should expect to find boom conditions in the manufacturing sector of the late medieval economy. To some extent, this was the case, but the evidence requires many qualifications. Prices of manufactured goods rose sharply throughout Europe, and the wages of artisans rose with them. In England, for example, if we take average prices during the period 1261–1350 as a base of 100, price levels for the next 50-year period, 1351–1400, are as follows. For metals, including lead, tin, solder, pewter, and brass, the index rises to 176; for textiles—here canvas, linen, and two types of woolen cloth—the index is 160; and finally, for agricultural implements, clouts, cloutnails, two types of wheels, ligatures, greatnails, hurdles, horseshoes, horseshoe nails, ploughshoes, and ploughshares, the index mounts to the enormous level of 235. These figures may be compared to a price index of 99 for barley, peas, wheat, and rye, calculated on the same basis, for the second half of the fourteenth century. In the same period, the wages of building craftsmen increased by nearly 50 per cent.

The statistics for England are more complete than those for any other country in the later Middle Ages, but sufficient, if less precise, evidence also remains to confirm the rapid rise of industrial prices elsewhere in Europe during the second half of the fourteenth century. At first sight, it would certainly appear that even if demographic decline precluded actual expansion, there was general and substantial prosperity throughout the urban communities of Europe for some time following the great population crisis. This is not, however, an adequate representation; more information concerning the duration and the precise incidence of this prosperity is required. In the first place, since part of the mechanism that created prosperity in the cities was the decline in the price of grain, it is necessary to consider more closely the relationship between agriculture and industry. A portion of the demand for manufactured goods emanated from the agricultural sector or from those who derived their incomes from that sector; as the economic conditions of the agricultural sector worsened under the pressures of overproduction and reduced markets, the potential rural market for manufactures contracted also. The gap between the prices of agricultural and of manufactured goods, the latter having risen sharply while the former remained stable or fell, could not long endure without bankrupting the countryside. As it was, the balance of payments between the two sectors already favored the towns. Towns paid less for food and sold their own products for more; as a result, money tended to accumulate in urban centers. Increased taxation and the migration of wealthy landlords to the more secure cities accelerated the outflow of rural funds and compounded the already observable pressures tending to demonetize the countryside by forcibly removing funds in the form of rents and taxes. When this began to happen, the rural portion of the demand for manufactures was undercut. That part of urban prosperity which had been based upon the divergence between the prices of manufactured and of agricultural products could last only so long as it took to drain the countryside of funds. In England, there is evidence that this had happened by the beginning of the fifteenth century; the price gap then closed, as the costs of manufactured goods fell in relation to agricultural prices. The mechanism that restored equilibrium between the two segments of the economy was, of course, more complex than the mere exhaustion of rural purchasing power. The stabilization and subsequent growth of population during the course of the fifteenth century altered the economic position of the agricultural producers and enlarged their markets. Also, as will be apparent later, broader issues of the international balance of payments exercised considerable influence upon urban prosperity in the later Middle Ages and may equally have acted to restore the balance between the agricultural and the manufacturing sectors.

Evaluation of the incidence of prosperity is of major importance in considering the temporary, post-plague affluence of the cities. Not all were equally favored by fortune's wand; some were altogether overlooked. Some areas, both geographical and occupational, benefited either at the expense of, or in comparison with, others. Here we encounter an extremely complex problem, whose complete solution would depend upon precise knowledge of the relative rates of productivity among industries, of shifts in tastes and fashions, of mortality rates by class of citizen, and of the relative durability of various types of goods. Needless to say, this sort of detailed evidence does not exist, but we may proceed, albeit with caution, on the basis of the fragmentary information that has survived.

Changes in the levels of consumption were accompanied by changes in the objects desired. Within the spectrum of manufactures, some goods enjoyed more elastic demand functions than did others. Northern Europeans, catching up to the Italians, became extraordinarily fashion-conscious during the second half of the fourteenth century, under the combined influence of southern styles and the momentarily increased financial affluence inherited by the survivors of the plagues. More luxurious clothes, jewelry, and the like tended to find better markets than the more traditional products for two reasons. On the one hand, it had become possible for more people to emulate the very rich of former times. On the other, the diminutive scale of production of the most exotic goods meant that such goods did not depend upon large markets before the plague and hence, that they were more or less insulated against the demographic pressures of the plague. Prosperity, for these producers, did not require a wide market composed of many consumers, but rather, a small market composed of rich consumers. Pestilence destroyed large numbers of people but it did not, in its initial phases, destroy wealth. Indeed, to the extent that the figures from

Albi reflect the general European experience, it would appear that the number of wealthy citizens in a position to buy costly luxuries grew as the total population declined. Consequently, luxury industries tended to flourish in the period following the demographic catastrophes, while those industries that had formerly served wide markets in a period of higher population density tended to fall rather quickly upon troubled times.

WOOL VERSUS SILK

The comparison of two textile industries, wool and silk, will serve to illustrate at once the shift in the relative positions of the two industries—the one a necessity, though with an important luxury component, the other a pure luxury trade—and also to bring out some of the geographical variation possible within the same industry. The great centers of the woolen industry during the thirteenth century had been the cities of Flanders, Ghent, Bruges and Ypres, and some major Italian cities such as Florence. Here the finest and most expensive cloth was produced and prepared for sale in an international market. These centers also produced ordinary cloth of low or medium quality, but the fame of the cities of the Low Countries, which extends back into the era of Charlemagne, had been earned in the manufacture of the finest cloth.

The arable terrain in Flanders was inadequate to supply either sufficient food for the cities or sufficient raw wool for the industry that supported the urban population. Consequently, wool was imported from England, worked up into cloth, and then exported to earn the funds necessary to pay for the imported food required by the densely populated urban areas. Flanders thus was vulnerable on two counts; if her food supply were cut off, she would starve; if her wool supply were cut off, she would also starve, but at a slower rate, since accumulated earnings could be used to avert disaster for a time. Unfortunately for the Flemish, the two strongest northern powers, France and England, were aware of the Flemish weaknesses —Edward I had capitalized upon them at the end of the thirteenth century—and both were at war after 1337. Edward III had formed an alliance with the King of Castile for the purpose of forcing Flanders to join England in the war against France. Castile, able to control domestic wool production through the Mesta, and England, the traditional supplier of Flemish industry, declared an embargo against the export of wool to Flanders and simultaneously encouraged foreign clothworkers to establish themselves in England. After the battle of Cadsand (1337), where they received a disastrous defeat at the hands of the English, the Flemish capitulated to the English demands, and the wool exports were resumed, but the terms of trade had weakened. Edward III was using wool exports as a source of finance for the war with France. Wool was taken in England through the rights of purveyance and sold abroad to raise funds. Italian bankers loaned money to the English crown against the security of subsidies based on the export of woolsacks. Finally, the Flemish were induced to make direct loans to Edward in order to assure continuance of the imports of the English wool so vital for their industrial existence. For Flanders, the collective impact of the beginning of the Hundred Years' War was sharply to increase wool prices, to magnify the hidden costs of mollifying the English, and to raise grave doubts concerning the future supply. It is little wonder, therefore, that Edward's policy, enforced as it was by trenchant national power, was successful in fostering an English woolen cloth industry. After the middle of the fourteenth century, England became a major exporter of cloth.

The Black Death of 1348–49 had several direct implications for the wool trade and for woolen production. First, the decrease in the population, particularly in the urban centers of the world, struck at the market for woolen cloth; fewer purchasers remained. This did not necessarily entail reduction in the prosperity of the remaining woolen manufacturers so long as the Death, as it probably did, struck producers and consumers with the same severity; but other factors were present to affect and distort this delicate balance. The second effect of the decline in population was a vast increase in the supply of raw wool available to the textile producers. Falling demand and falling prices for the basic grains and rising labor costs led farmers to convert arable land to pasture. Throughout Europe, raw wool became more plentiful, and as it did, the dangers of over-

GRAPH V Trends in the Cloth Trade: Marseille, Florence, Ypres, and England

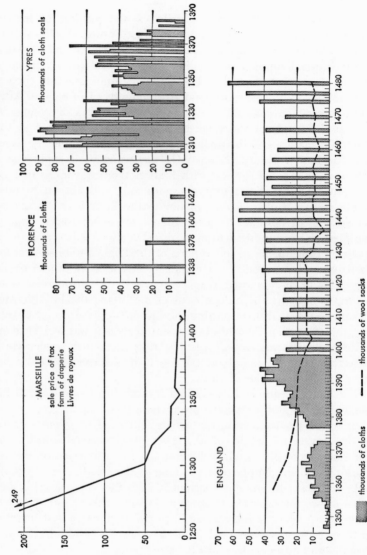

production for markets, reduced by the plague, became real. Graph V describes the trends in the woolen industry in several major textile centers of the fourteenth and fifteenth centuries.

The rapid development of the English cloth industry is immediately visible on the graph; from the thirteen-forties, when virtually no cloth was exported, the shipments rise to almost 45,000 cloths per year in the last decade of the fourteenth century. This remarkable performance has often been cited as evidence of both general industrial growth and of a rapid rise in prosperity after the plague, but it is well to consider the broader international costs of its attainment before drawing such conclusions. In the second decade of the fourteenth century, the figures for Ypres indicate that cloth production reached more than 90,000 cloths annually in the best years. In the late thirteen-fifties and -sixties, however, output hovered around 50,000 pieces, and by the last three decades of the century, the average level had fallen below 25,000. The decline in the average annual cloth output at Ypres thus appears to have exceeded 60,000 cloths over the course of the century. Edward III had been triumphantly successful in destroying the Flemish industry and in transferring part of it to England, but the Flemish depression must moderate the claims permitted to the English success. The English accomplishment lay in the transplantation of an industry rather than in the creation of a new area of industrial enterprise; save from the viewpoint of English national power, it was a rather sterile achievement. In the face of a declining world market—the decline at the city of Ypres alone was greater than the entire English export trade—England, through the exercise of national power and

GRAPH V

SOURCES: E. Baratier and F. Reynaud, *Histoire du Commerce de Marseille*, Vol. II, Librairie Plon, Paris, 1951, for Marseille; R. S. Lopez, "Hard Times and Investment in Culture," *op. cit.*, for Florence; H. van Werveke, "De omvang van de Ieperse lakenproductie in de veertiende eeuw," *Mededelingen, K. Vlaamse Acad. voor Wetensch., Letteren en schone Kunsten van Belgie*, 1947, for Ypres; C. M. Cipolla, "The Decline of Italy," *Economic History Review*, V (1952); E. M. Carus-Wilson, "Trends in the Export of English Woolens in the Fourteenth Century," *Economic History Review*, 1950, period to 1399; M. M. Postan, "The Trade of Medieval Europe: the North," *The Cambridge Economic History of Europe*, Cambridge, 1952, for England after 1399.

the economic control of raw materials, had gained regional economic prosperity at the expense of Flanders.

Even within the totality of the English woolen industry, however, not all facets flourished. The amount of raw wool exported decreased rapidly after 1350 as a portion, but only a portion, of the domestic clip was converted into cloth by the nascent textile industry. A sack of wool was sufficient to make slightly more than four cloths; thus, the decline in wool exports—more than 30,000 sacks between 1350 and 1430—would have been equivalent to something on the order of 120,000 cloths. If the 40,000 cloths actually exported in 1430 are subtracted from this figure, it appears that a trade gap of approximately 80,000 cloths had arisen. The decrease in the amount of wool sold internationally achieves major social significance when we recall that one of the remedies employed by desperate farmers to shore up their declining revenues was the conversion of arable land to pasture for sheep. Some of the wool, no longer being exported, was undoubtedly consumed domestically; however, taking into account the new production from recently converted lands and the decrease in the domestic population, it seems unlikely that the entire margin could have been absorbed at the old prices. It is noteworthy that the sharp fall in wool exports after 1390 coincided with an equally sharp drop in cloth exports and, by the beginning of the fifteenth century, with a decrease in wool prices. Even in England, the first decades of the fifteenth century were a time of retreat from the early achievements of the textile industry.

The English woolen industry was at once more mechanized and less localized than its continental counterpart. The use of fulling mills for matting and shrinking the woven cloth had been on the increase since the end of the twelfth century, but, with the growth of the English cloth industry in the fourteenth century, more mills and more water-power sites were required. These requirements could not always be met in the old textile cities, so the industry was compelled to move abroad into the outer reaches of England that were better endowed with streams. New cloth centers grew up in East Anglia, Yorkshire, and the West Country, drawing industry away from the old centers. Producers in the traditional centers felt themselves threatened with obsolescence and, in some cases, attempted through restrictive guild and urban legislation to reverse the economic tide and to force the textile industry to remain in the old cities despite the technological advantages implicit in their transfer to the country. London clothiers and fullers, for example, had attempted from the turn of the thirteenth century to hold back the change to the use of mechanical fulling mills, in order to preserve the urban industry. The traditional technique of fulling by hand—or more accurately, by foot, since the earliest process entailed trampling the cloth in a foul mixture of alum, urine, and fuller's earth—could be undertaken in the cities because it did not require running streams. England, however, was the beneficiary of a rising textile industry and could afford to be somewhat benevolent in the face of change. In spite of all local attempts to restrict production and to prevent change, the old centers decayed and new ones were formed. Over the course of the late thirteenth and early fourteenth centuries, the textile industry moved away from eastern England; the economic pressures were too great, and the efforts to resist the new mechanical methods died with the guilds in such old cloth centers as Oxford, York, and Lincoln. The new industry, more vital, more inventive, and far more widely dispersed geographically, did not submit so readily to restrictive practices during its period of rapid development.

On the other hand, the emergence of England as a prominent cloth exporter in the world markets brought her into direct competition with the older suppliers. This confrontation, occurring in a time of falling population and declining markets, tended to cause a world-wide reaction and withdrawal into restrictionism. The great Flemish cloth towns made every effort to conserve their status in the textile industry. The continental industry had always been centered in the towns, and consequently it was more closely integrated from spinner to finisher than was the English industry. From the urban viewpoint in Flanders, more was at stake, and more concentrated political power was available for mobilization in defense of the textile industry against the adverse winds of the fourteenth century. The major textile cities throughout Flanders passed regulations to prohibit the manufacture of cloth outside the city walls. On an even more grandiose scale, in response to the English embargo on the export of raw wool after 1336, the major Flemish towns Ghent, Ypres, and Bruges banded together and pooled their collective resources for the defense of their trade. Their immediate problem was to reopen the route for English wool; this was accomplished by 1339, when the towns allied with the English after driving out their Count, Louis of Nevers, who remained loyal to the French king. The towns then found time to turn to more local issues, in particular the competition from other textile producers within Flanders. Through collective action, the towns were able to establish political control over the Flemish hinterland and to destroy or limit cloth production that appeared to be in competition with their own in the weakening international markets. Armed craftsmen from the great cities exercised main force to break looms and to destroy the tenter frames and vats of the fullers of the countryside. Ever closer attention was paid to each violation of the rigid statutes imposed in the self-interest of producers in the large centers. Within those centers, producers attempted further to insulate themselves from competition. Guild regulations tightened, and as fees and standards were arbitrarily raised, it became increasingly difficult to join. Lacking the new industrial growth that coincided with the decay of the old centers in England, the Flemish cities responded to world population decline, falling markets, and new competition through increasingly monopolistic practices. Inevitably, since they could only hope to control local trade, their policies were inadequate to cope with an international crisis. Their failure is written in the cascading figures of the cloth production at Ypres; the figures are paralleled by comparable declines in the other cities of Flanders.

In Florence also, the fourteenth century was a period of recession in the woolen industry. Woolen production in 1338 reached an annual total of almost 80,000 cloths but 40 years later, in 1378, it had fallen to less than 24,000 cloths. It is worth observing that this decline, more than 50,000 cloths in a single city, by itself more than matched the entire growth in English cloth exports over the course of the fourteenth century; the decline at Ypres was even greater. In Florence, as in Flanders, the reaction to recession was strong, restrictive, and sometimes violent. The figures that survive for the year 1378 emanate from the demands of cloth workers, then in a state of active revolt, who were insisting that a minimum level of 24,000 cloths be produced annually. The impoverished clothworkers, weavers, and fullers sought to wrest control of the city from the urban patriciate during the years 1378–82, but despite some temporary success, they were repressed, although many of their demands for protectionist policies were met. In 1393, a prohibitive duty was levied against almost all foreign cloth, and a series of defensive measures for the preservation of trade secrets and the withholding of strategic raw materials from competitors followed. During the early fifteenth century, some improvement occurred in the Florentine woolen industry, but it seems to have been due mostly to the collapse of the Flemish manufactures. Flemings emigrated to Italy as well as to England, and with them, the number of Florentine textile firms grew by 50 per cent between 1427 and 1480. Output, on the other hand, does not seem to have kept pace with the increase in the number of firms; according to the Italian historian Gino Luzzatto, it never surpassed 30,000 cloths per year during the entire course of the fifteenth century.

The Florentine industry did not respond to crisis only through restrictionism, however. It is noteworthy that the type of product made was adjusted to fit the market—a creative response, at the same time that the town undertook the more sterile exercise of attempting to adjust the market through legislation. Fewer cloths were produced, but they were more luxurious materials, manufactured from the finest of the English wools and from the expensive, short-stapled, merino wool from Spain and sometimes, after the fifteenth century, from Italy itself. The price of the newer cloth of high quality was more than double that of the former product, so that the economic loss that followed the reduction in output was at least partially compensated for by the increased revenue per unit sold. On the other hand, it is doubtful that the production of fewer, but more expensive, cloths represented an ideal solution for the problems confronting the workers. Production of expensive cloth assured markets among the very rich and among the beneficiaries of newly inherited wealth after the plagues; it did not provide sufficient opportunities for employment to compensate the poor of Florence, as their own brief gains from the plague were dissipated over time.

It would be misleading to suggest that the only, or even the chief source of trouble for the older textile-producing centers was the

competition of the English. Despite unfavorable conditions generally and insurmountable problems in particular regions such as
Flanders, other areas of Europe began to prosper and to develop
cloth industries at almost the same time as did England. In the
north, Brabant and Holland were able to benefit from the decay of
the Flemish industry and to capture for themselves some of the
trade lost by the southern lowlands. In both regions, favorable political conditions contributed greatly to the economic achievements.
Brabant, under the guidance of a series of wise counts, was able to
capitalize upon her status as an imperial fief and to maintain a
profitable neutrality during the Anglo-French struggles of the fourteenth century. She curried favor with the English in order to keep
her wool supplies open during the several embargoes placed against
the Flemish and, at the same time, was able to maintain commercial
contact with the French. Brabant's imperial status preserved for her
the markets of Germany, while shrewd manipulation of her position on the fringes of the Anglo-French conflict allowed her to mul-
tiply the advantages gained from each combatant.

Holland also gained from her avoidance of war, but in this case,
it was a northern war that was evaded. The endeavor to control
Flanders economically had led the Hanseatic league to place an
embargo on food exports to the Flemish after 1356, adding to the
already severe difficulties of that troubled region and simultaneously increasing the potential for Dutch growth, by weakening the
competitive strength of Flanders. The Hanse, however, certainly
had neither foreseen nor intended this result and, for the remainder
of its effective commercial life, sought to destroy the Dutch threat
to its commercial supremacy in the north. In the long run, its efforts were frustrated, both by problems of internal organization
within the Hanse and by increasingly difficult external relations
with the emerging national powers of northern Europe. The Hanse
was too loose an organization to establish and maintain monopolistic power for any extended period of time under conditions of
political and economic stress, but as the later Middle Ages wore on,
the stress increased. Wars with Denmark in 1367–70 and in the
fourteen-twenties deflected Hanseatic energies from the task of sup-
pressing the Dutch, while the defeat of the Teutonic Knights, the
traditional military arm of the Hanse, at the battle of Tannenberg

in 1410 weakened Hanseatic military and commercial strength in the Polish hinterlands. The northeastern termini of the Hanseatic trade routes were thenceforth increasingly subject to the challenge of external competition. After 1430, when Philip the Good, Duke of Burgundy, gained Holland through inheritance, the political and economic position of the Dutch was enhanced by the considerable and growing strength of the Burgundian state. Dutch fortune waxed as the Hanse waned. In the late fourteenth and early fifteenth centuries, cloth from Amsterdam, Leyden, Haarlem, and Rotterdam began to infiltrate the northern markets that once had been the exclusive province of the Hanse. By 1441, the Dutch had won a treaty giving them free access to the Baltic.

In southern Germany also, the cloth industry developed rapidly after the late fourteenth century as producers found that they could capitalize upon the still active markets of central and eastern Europe. Indeed, both the Dutch and the Brabantines, from the north, and the clothiers of Nuremberg and Augsburg, from the south, were seeking out the same markets or at least markets that remained active for similar reasons. Money, once the initial effects of the plague had passed, became increasingly scarce in northwestern Europe during the late fourteenth and early fifteenth centuries so markets in these regions tended to contract. In central Europe, particularly in Hungary, on the contrary, mining remained fairly active, and consequently there appears to have been a greater quantity of specie to sustain trade. Further, the fur trade of north central Europe and of the Black Sea region of Russia was growing during the later Middle Ages, and it provided additional funds that could be used by northerners to purchase fine cloth and Mediterranean luxuries. The south Germans benefited from their location on the north–south axis of this trade and could add their own cloth to the northward flow of Mediterranean goods. The Dutch and the Brabantines found equal profit in selling their goods in this market, although in their case, it was reached through the northern sea lanes. Further, as we observed during the discussion of agriculture, parts of eastern Europe during the fourteenth and fifteenth centuries were just emerging from the effects of the disasters suffered by them in the thirteenth century. Population was probably increasing in these regions, and combined with greater availability of money

and improved levels of monetary sophistication, the growth in population tended to provide stronger markets for western cloth.

But developments in Holland, Brabant, and southern Germany
were not sufficient to replace the older industries that had fallen
victim to the economic contraction of the late fourteenth century.
True, they rose from the ruins of the earlier cloth centers, but a
considerable time elapsed before they were able to generate anything like the outputs attained by the older towns when they were
in their prime. The Brabantine industry probably grew faster and
further than the industries of Holland or Germany, but it was not
until well into the fifteenth century that any of the three regions
acquired the international recognition and importance formerly
held by the old Flemish industry. By then, almost a hundred years
had passed since the great pestilence of the fourteenth century;
Europe had begun to recover as population grew, as old markets
revived and new ones were discovered in the Atlantic, as the Hundred Years' War drew to an end, and as precious metals became
more abundant. In the late fourteenth and early fifteenth centuries,
however, these changes had not yet occurred, and the slow growth
of the new textile centers remained inadequate to compensate for
the contraction and collapse of the old. Some geographical adjustments were made in response to the crises of the later Middle Ages,
and some credit must be allotted to the new centers for partially
stemming the fall, but contraction was the dominant theme in the
woolen industry for many decades following the first incidence of
the Black Death. Given the economic conditions of the time, the
retreat from the mass market, or its medieval equivalent, into the
production of the most expensive luxuries—the pattern followed
by the shrewd and market-sensitive clothiers of Florence—probably
was the best-advised policy, but as the rebellious workers who
joined the Ciompi uprising in 1378 well knew, it did not re-estab-
lish the former prosperity of the textile centers.

Even within the luxury markets, competition for the consumers'
cash was increased by the introduction of new products; from the
beginning of the fourteenth century, the best woolens yielded their
almost exclusive position as items of conspicuous consumption to
a varied array of silks, brocades, damasks, and velvets. Silk had
long been known in the west, but its use became ever more popu-

lar, first in the affluent cities of the south and then, rather later, after the beginning of the fourteenth century, in the countries of northwestern Europe. The market for silk had traditionally been composed of the nobility and higher clergy, but, during the late fourteenth century, it deepened considerably. On the one hand, the effects of the plague, by raising both the amounts and the numbers of legacies made to the Church, often directly specifying the purchase of vestments, increased the ecclesiastical demand for silk. On the other hand, the reduced price of food and the direct inheritance effects of the plague in the urban communities of the north heightened the bourgeois demand for the finest fabrics, and these included silks, brocades, and even cloth of gold and silver. From the time of the first great plague, growing quantities of silk appeared in the hands of the merchant class of London; in one not atypical case, probate records show a legacy containing, among other more banal items of real estate and money, a bedcovering replete with a stripe of Florentine silk down the center. As the century progressed, more and more references to silken goods, purses, belts, girdles, and hoods, appear in the probate records of the English upper bourgeoisie as well as in numerous literary and municipal documents in France and Germany.

Although the market for silk was developing rapidly, the supply remained limited in relation to the demand despite some expansion during the fourteenth and fifteenth centuries. In the thirteenth century, the Italian town of Lucca had been the center of the silk industry, but by the end of the first decade of the fourteenth century, civil disturbances in Lucca had driven Luchese silkworkers to seek refuge in many other northern Italian towns, particularly Venice, Florence, Bologna, and Milan, and thus their industrial skills were dispersed to these areas. The silk industry required highly skilled labor, and by the end of the thirteenth century, it employed labor-saving equipment in the silk-throwing machine that enabled one worker to do the work formerly performed by scores. Thus, the growth of the silk industry did not provide large-scale employment opportunities, nor was it capable of readily absorbing workers displaced from the declining woolen industry. It did, however, constitute a substantial source of foreign earnings in those towns where it became established, and it yielded very high returns to the chosen few who possessed the proper skill and equipment to work in the silk trade.

Even if it had been technologically possible to increase the potential output of silk by training labor and thus bypassing the shortage of skilled workers, the difficulties in procuring raw materials would have saved the industry from the blight of overproduction. As we have seen, the revival of northern Italian agriculture witnessed the cultivation of many luxury crops whose sale at high prices was assured, while the decline of southern Italy's wheat farming has led to substantially the same result in that area. In both regions, sericulture expanded during the fourteenth and fifteenth centuries. Despite these gains, Italian production of raw silk remained inadequate, and imports from Spain, Asia Minor, and even from China were required in order to make up the deficit. During the fifteenth century, however, political circumstance cut off the Asian routes and kept the price of silk high. The rise of the Ming dynasty in China, after 1368, ended the friendly trade relations between western Europe and Asia that had prevailed during the Mongol period and had allowed Marco Polo to travel unmolested throughout the Far East. Further, the growing strength of the Ottoman Turks in the eastern Mediterranean acted to unsettle the overland silk trade in the Black Sea region and ultimately, in the mid-fifteenth century, across all Asia Minor.

Spared from the dangers of overproduction and lucky enough, due to the special circumstances of the late fourteenth century, to enjoy a growing market while the demand for other products fell, the silk industry was one of the most profitable enterprises of the later Middle Ages. We are unusually fortunate in possessing figures that allow us to compare profits in the wool and the silk industries during the same period of the fifteenth century, in the same city, and under essentially the same management. Raymond de Roover has published the accounts of the Medici Bank, whose headquarters were in Florence, for the years 1435–51.[2] At this time, the Medici operated two wool shops and one silk shop. The combined capital of the two wool shops on March 25, 1451, amounted to 10,000 florins; over the 17-year span from 1435 to this date, the profits came

---

[2] Raymond de Roover, *The Rise and Decline of the Medici Bank, 1397–1494* (Cambridge, Mass.: Harvard University Press, 1963).

to 10,373 florins or 103.7 per cent. In the silk shop, the capital at the same date was 7,200 florins, while the profits totaled 19,126 florins, or 265.6 per cent for the 17 recorded years. The silk shop thus yielded an average return more than two and one-half times greater than that of the wool shops, even without taking into account a reorganization in the year 1441 that greatly increased the capital investment in silk. If the appropriate adjustment were made for this reorganization, the average capital employed by the silk shop during the period would appear smaller, and consequently the percentage return on the investment would be even greater. Comparison of the two industrial undertakings of the Medici confirms in microcosm, then, what we already have observed. The woolen industry survived the crises of the fourteenth century, but it had lost its energy; profits, a bare 6 per cent per year, were not impressive by medieval standards, and markets were slow for all but the finest cloth. But in the silk industry, the pinnacle of luxury production, profits remained high, at 16 per cent a year, and the industry flourished; in fact, the silk shop was one of the last of the Medici ventures to remain profitable at the time of the firm's dissolution in the last decade of the fifteenth century. Success, in the economy of the later Middle Ages, came to those who produced exotic, expensive, and socially conspicuous goods on a small scale, although output was often greater than it had been in the early fourteenth century. Since production had never been large, the market, instead of being spoiled by the depopulation, was improved by the inheritance effects of the plagues and by the desire of many of the survivors to live well, even though death was an ever-present guest at the feast.

RESTRICTION, REGULATION, AND PESSIMISM

Mixed evidence—the rise of the wool trade in England in contrast with its fall in Flanders, the over-all decline in woolen production in contrast with the rise of the silk industry—has led economic historians to make differing judgments regarding the economic condition of the later Middle Ages. Areas of growth undoubtedly existed, but they often lay in specialized, highly skilled, small industries, whereas in the older and larger industries, contraction was the rule. It is, perhaps, difficult to strike the correct balance in every case, but on the whole, it would appear that contraction among the great industries generally outweighed the advances in the smaller ones. Statistics of output, per capita production, and personal income are virtually nonexistent, but contemporary attitudes toward the economic environment of the later Middle Ages offer a fruitful source of information. Were producers cheerful and sanguine about the present and future state of their businesses? If so, we might be tempted to side with those who see the later Middle Ages as a period of prosperity or at least of rapid transformation leading to new and greater heights of prosperity. If not—if instead, the typical entrepreneur expressed fear and gloom and strove to hoard the last scraps of affluence by policies of jealous exclusiveness—then we might well take the negative side of the prosperity thesis. Let us look at the evidence.

We have already observed that rigid trade regulations and restrictionism dominated the economic policies of those towns and regions whose textile industries were no longer prosperous, but such policies were not limited only to cloth or to the cloth towns. The history of the late fourteenth and early fifteenth centuries is fraught with intra-urban struggles between local producers and guildsmen on one side and the patriciate and merchant class, which had long been predominant, on the other. Under the pressures of economic contraction, swift growth and consolidation of guilds occurred among the lesser artisanate during the later Middle Ages, and with that growth came demands for protection against economic adversity through strengthened municipal regulation. It was not long before such demands, tantamount to the demand for true political power within the urban communities, brought the lesser artisans into conflict with the greater merchants and the hautebourgeoisie. In many cases, open revolt ensued, as with the Ciompi in Florence and as in the Pan-European spate of urban revolts that marked the history of the late thirteen-seventies and early thirteeneighties throughout the west.

In France, the struggle within the cities frequently worked to the long-run advantage of the monarchy: first by weakening the old power structure; then either, in exceptional cases, by substituting a new or, more normally, by dividing and thus cancelling the effective force of the old structure through the creation of a parallel leadership, composed of the more easily controlled lesser artisanate. Although urban rioting pushed this process along when it occurred, it seems to have had more complex origins than class struggle alone. In France, urban disorder was associated with royal taxation, with the class struggle between the great and the small, and with the urgent need for protection from the effects of economic contraction. During the early thirteen-eighties, the immediate provocation for revolt was often the imposition, or rather the reimposition, of the hearth taxes that had been canceled by Charles V on the morning of his death, September 16, 1380. Urban unrest met brutal suppression by the power-hungry regents of the young Charles VI, and with the repression came fines, restoration of the taxes, and loss of municipal liberties. Since a city which had rebeled had violated the sanctions of custom and law in the first instance, once the rebellion was crushed, the city could find little support from those sanctions to aid it in reclaiming privileges lost during the suppression of the revolt. Often, the town oligarchies defended the authority of the king against the unruly and dangerous lower classes, but this did not, in France, suffice to preserve urban liberties. Typically, the towns were punished as towns, without specific concern for locating the actual perpetrators of the revolt, and thus rebellion served as an excuse for reducing the power of the oligarchy. Indeed, concessions were often made, after a time, to the demands of the lower ranks of urban society—artisans in the local crafts—and these were often of an economic nature. It is important to avoid here the temptation of excessive historical compression; the pattern—revolt, suppression, loss of privileges, and subsequent alteration of the intraurban power balance—is, in some senses, an abstraction and a model, but many variations and omissions occurred in the sequence, while the period required for its completion varies from a few years to many decades. The revolts of the thirteen-eighties were powerless, by themselves, to reverse totally the course of history or to invert the status of the cities. It is true, however, that during the course of the fourteenth and fifteenth centuries, particularly during the reigns of Charles VII and Louis XI, many royal concessions were granted to local craft guilds. Concessions from the French monarchy, however, at least in terms of their intent and their welfare content, were frequently on a par with the cheese in a mousetrap. By encouraging and confirming charters for local craft guilds, the monarchy gained both allies and administrations within the cities that could be used to supplement, challenge, or control the ruling oligarchies. At the same time, by establishing that the granting of guild charters was a prerogative of the king, the monarchy, imperceptibly at first, altered the whole fabric of society and began to transmute the legal basis of corporate existence. So long as guilds existed, as they had in the thirteenth century, as simple associations of individuals, each transferring the rights and privileges of his individual existence to the corporate structure, the guild was both outside the monarchy's direct control and, to some extent, defended by those premises of divine and natural law and those institutions, such as the Church, which supported the role of the individual. Once the king had established first the desirability and then the necessity of royal charters, the guilds became *"choses du roi,"* "things of the king"; collectively, they formed a powerful institution of political control and of royal authority. The process took several centuries, but it began in the later Middle Ages, particularly in the fifteenth century, when many manufacturers were impelled by the pressures of a declining economy to seek royal aid in defending their markets and extending their monopoly powers.

Examples are myriad, but a few will suffice to demonstrate the desire for royal aid. In 1375, the tanners of the town of Sens obtained a royal charter to allow them to crush the competition that arose from the presence of independent leather workers. Seven years later, the Rouenaise vintners sought royal support to extend their monopoly throughout Normandy. In 1398, Norman ship packers and loaders were organized into a guild by royal charter. During the reigns of Charles VII and Louis XI, the creation of guilds and, in the case of pre-existing guilds, the confirmation of their statutes, rose to record levels. Charles VII established new guilds in a vast number of cities beyond Paris—among them Montpellier, Poitiers, Bourges, Issoudun, Tours, La Rochelle, Rouen, Gisors, Bordeaux, and Marseille. Louis XI issued more than 60 ordinances conveying the royal sanction to old guilds and creating new ones.

As a political conception, the idea of utilizing guilds for the control of urban complexes and economic activity may be traced as far back as the late Roman Empire. As a concrete political fact, the actual utilization of guilds in this manner was largely an accomplishment of the French monarchy—an accomplishment that in time would provide the economic power and the financial resources required to sustain the splendor of the *Grand Siècle*. The events that enabled the French kings to gain such broad control of the guilds were multiple, but the economic problems afflicting the industries of the later Middle Ages certainly played an important role. The ordinances that granted or confirmed guild charters were frequently prefaced by a statement to the effect that the king, out of love for his subjects, has graciously granted the request of such-and-such a group of craftsmen for permission to form a guild, or to control the trade in a certain commodity or region. The grant of royal privilege was indeed valuable—it was often costly as well—since it provided broader and stronger protection against competition than that available from any other political body, urban or feudal. Royal sanctions became ever more desirable in the face of declining markets, and hence economic contraction led to an increased willingness on the part of the craftsmen to seek aid from the king. With royal permission in hand, the guilds could indulge their tastes for monopolistic practices and jealous exclusiveness and, at the same time, use part of the monopoly revenues which they earned with the king's help to pay him for the privileges which he had granted. Restrictionism thus grew swiftly during the late fourteenth and early fifteenth centuries, and since the costly privileges had to be paid for, it is likely that the costs were passed along to consumers and hopeful apprentices in the guise of higher quality standards and stricter apprenticeship requirements. That which the king had created, however, was the king's to destroy. Royal privilege was not permitted to become a blanket grant covering any whim or abuse desired by the guildsmen. Close control over the guilds followed their charters; royal agents supervised the election of officers, controlled standards, regulated prices, established and sometimes loosened the levels of qualification for admission to the guilds, and created new masters at will. As the monarchy grew in strength, the controls became increasingly heavyhanded and free from constraint; from the fifteenth century on, they were often imposed without even the formality of consulting the officers of the guilds.

Considerable space has been allotted to the development of guilds in France both because of their close connection with the monarchy and because of their value as an example of the degree to which royal authority could be asserted over industry during the economic and demographic contractions of the late fourteenth and fifteenth centuries. The pattern is not unique to France, however, for similar developments may be traced throughout Europe, particularly in Spain, where the growing strength of the central monarchy supported, and was in turn supported by, the guilds until the union of the crowns of Aragon and Castile in the late fifteenth century rendered the Spanish crown the dominant giant of the sixteenth century. In Germany, on the other hand, the absence of strong central government virtually eliminated the possibility that ties between Crown and guild would develop along French lines. In Germany, as elsewhere, regulations multiplied and monopolistic practices grew in response to the difficult times, but the policies remained mere urban particularism, more or less specific in each individual town, without ever being transformed into a wider system of political and economic control. In a few instances, particularly in the south, economic dislocations and shifting patterns of trade altered the internal political balance in the German towns and produced a stronger but less, rather than more, provincial defense of vested urban interests. Augsburg, for example, benefited both from the collapse of the older northern cloth industry formerly centered in Flanders and from its location as an intermediary between the temporarily favored regions of central and eastern Europe and the Mediterranean luxury trade. The merchants' and weavers' guilds, supplied with expatriate skilled labor from Flanders and with rich markets to the northeast, successfully gained control of the town. These merchants naturally sought continuation of the international cloth trade, which had enabled them to overcome the traditional local patriciate, whose political power had depended upon agrarian incomes, a weak reed during the agricultural crisis of the late fourteenth century. In this case, enhanced economic opportunity strengthened the guilds while the widespread demographic and agrarian slump undermined the patriciate. The net effect—the extension of the political and economic power of the guilds—was identical with the common pattern found throughout the industrial structure of western Europe. In the more usual case, however, the motivating force sprang from the desperate endeavor of the guilds, particularly the artisan guilds, to save themselves from ruin in the face of crumbling markets, shifting patterns of trade, and demands for higher wages by the laborers, whose numbers were reduced by the plague.

With few exceptions, the attitude of merchants and craftsmen during the later fourteenth and early fifteenth centuries was one of pessimism. It found social expression in restrictionism, in monopolistic arrangements of every kind that could be conceived in the fertile minds of late medieval guildsmen, and in attempts to preserve markets and limit outputs by any available means, even by outright violence and forcible suppression of competition. This was particularly true in the more economically developed regions of the late medieval world, where there was the most to be lost and the economic structure was most vulnerable. Even when the pattern exhibits some significant variation, as in the case of Augsburg, the explanation seems ready to hand; even the greatest and most profound economic depressions do not produce utter ruin for all. Contraction was accompanied by major dislocations in the older industrial and agrarian structure, but these very dislocations provided, in their turn, unique opportunities for a few specialized industries in a few fortunate regions. Silk benefited from the concentration of purchasing power resultant upon the inheritance effects of the plague. Southern Germany's advance was due to a combination of factors: central Europe to some extent retained or recovered its prosperity and population while the west declined, providing markets both for Mediterranean luxuries that passed through the region and for the goods of southern Germany itself; mining remained more active in central Europe and hence fostered wider trade by supplying the necessary precious metal. As a result, guild development in southern Germany in the later Middle Ages was somewhat different from that of the remainder of Europe and more closely akin to that of western Europe during the affluent thirteenth century than in the difficult fourteenth and fifteenth centuries.

Exceptions, however, do not destroy the general rule. The fourteenth and fifteenth centuries, broadly considered, constitute a period of increasing restrictionism typified by policies of jealous exclusiveness among merchants and craftsmen alike. Consequently, while giving due attention to the occasional nodes of prosperity and the few remaining centers of affluence, it would appear evident that merchant opinion on the whole provides support for the view that the few new opportunities that opened up as a result of plague, famine, war, and depopulation were not sufficient to compensate for the losses sustained by the older, greater industries.

It is not presently possible to pursue the course of each separate industrial activity during the later Middle Ages in such detail as would be required for a definitive evaluation of the depth and incidence of the economic contraction, but the comparison between the woolen and silk industries reveals certain significant shifts in taste and a tendency toward luxury consumption. One additional factor that affected the aggregate demand for goods remains to be considered. In an era when credit instruments in most regions remained relatively primitive, mining was very closely connected with the money supply and, consequently, with the level of effective demand for goods and services. For the same reasons, the output of the mines, of course, was equally important in influencing the flow of international trade, but that aspect of the industry will be deferred until the following chapter.

MINING

For the moment, however, let us consider the status of the mining industry at the close of the Middle Ages in relation to its earlier levels of technology and output. Medieval mining, although it had experienced a considerable boom during the thirteenth century, was technologically far inferior to the mining undertaken in classical antiquity. Mines were typically shallow—often no more than bell-shaped pits worked by two or three men; often they were simply trenches whose size was determined by the physical strength of the miner. Courage was a more important quality for a miner than engineering skill. The ability to delve hundreds of feet below the surface had been lost since late Roman times, and although there is some evidence of the use of more advanced techniques in central Europe during the high Middle Ages, such methods were limited to that region and, even there, to the precious metals. This was natural enough, for as mine depth increased, the costs of extracting the ore rose and, in all probability, rose more than proportionally. A surface pit could normally be dug without fear of flooding, but even if the worst happened, it could economically be abandoned as soon as the water table was reached. The engineering problems in deeper mines were far more complex; timbers had to be cut and fitted along the shaft to prevent collapse, and adits had to be dug, or drainage engines constructed, to remove the water as it flowed into the mine. Clearly, the deeper the shaft, the greater was the cost and, more significantly, the greater was the cost per unit of ore. Only the most precious metals could sustain these heavy expenditures, and even in this branch of mining, the limits of profitability were quickly reached.

In mining, as in agriculture, the early fourteenth century was a period when the sins of the fathers were visited upon the sons. Exploitation of the mineral wealth of Europe had progressed for several centuries under a relatively constant technology, and consequently, diminishing returns afflicted miners everywhere. Further, by about 1300, the eastward expansion of Europe had virtually ceased, and consequently the opening up of new mines in lands newly added to the European hegemony faltered. Old mines were exhausted, and new deposits were less easily discovered.

In England, the silver mines of Devon, which had produced an average of about £900 of silver annually during the last decade of the thirteenth century, were yielding no more than £70 per year by 1347. During the interim of the early fourteenth century, the Italian Frescobaldi company was driven to relinquish control of the mines because their profitability had declined to such a degree that the company could no longer afford to pay the royalties due to the king for the right to exploit the mines.

In other regions also, particularly the older and once richer mining centers, the technological limits of mineral exploitation were reached by the middle of the fourteenth century. Silver mining was especially vulnerable throughout Germany, Hungary, and central Europe. A few regions—Bosnia and Serbia—appear to have experienced a modest increase in gold production, but even in this metal, the over-all trend throughout the late fourteenth and early fifteenth centuries was downward. Throughout much of central Europe, political instability exacerbated the downward trend already caused by overexploitation of mineral wealth under a stagnant technology. Bohemia, one of the richest mining centers of the high Middle Ages, suffered heavily from the political consequences of religious schism. John Hus—heretic or reformer, depending on one's point of view, but certainly the symbol of Bohemian national sentiment—had journeyed to the Council of Constance in 1415 under the protection of an imperial safe-conduct. His immediate imprisonment and subsequent death at the stake is not directly relevant here, but the political cost to Bohemia was twenty years of destructive war as the Holy Roman Emperor, Sigismund, sought to suppress the revolution that followed his betrayal of Hus. Terrorism and scorched-earth policies conjoined to deepen the impact of the war, while the equality of the match produced a near stalemate—a stalemate of swirling destruction. Mining towns throughout Saxony and Bohemia were devastated, skilled miners scattered, and production curtailed.

After 1300, then, many factors combined to reduce Europe's output of precious metals. Population growth rates first slowed and then, with the appearance of the bubonic plague, turned negative; migration and expansion faltered, and new mines were less readily discovered. Old mines failed and even those that remained productive became more difficult to operate as drainage machinery pushed up costs. The decline in the aggregate production of monetary metals undoubtedly had more generalized effects, both by limiting the possible increase in, or by lowering levels of, aggregate demand for goods and services and by reducing one of the balancing items in international trade. In itself, however, the reduction in the output of monetary metal would not have produced immediate and serious consequences in a closed and tightly circumscribed regional economy. Its ultimate importance may be understood and evaluated only after study of the patterns of international trade and recognition that the economy of Renaissance Europe was indeed an international economy.

4

The International Economy

ORIGINS

Even during the most dismal and bleak centuries of the Middle
Ages, long-distance trade was undertaken by those intrepid adventurers who were prepared to risk the dangers of sea or overland
travel in search of the great rewards afar, which were kept at high
levels by the very dangers that turned away the fainthearted. By the
beginning of the thirteenth century, however, trade had become
more a way of life than uncertain adventure, and regular institutions and trade routes had been devised by medieval merchants for
their convenience and profit. As Europe emerged from the troubled
centuries that followed the collapse of Charlemagne's empire, a few
regions at first slowly found peace, or at least some degree of political security, and then in time, whole countries came to experience
the benefits of an increasingly stable political order. With greater
security came greater opportunities for trade. Thus, the early unifi-
cation of Flanders under relatively strong Counts allowed increased
exchange and production of goods. To the south, the expansion of
European political power in the Mediterranean with the clearing
of the Arabs and, ultimately with the Crusades, into the Levantine
coast itself, served to rekindle the embers of the active trade conducted in antiquity, which even the Arabs' partial domination of
the Mediterranean was impotent to extinguish totally. In central
France, the Counts of Champagne had discovered the profitability
of encouraging merchants and thus expanding their own sources of
revenue. Consequently, the French counts sought to extend their
own political influence by bargaining with other feudatories so as

116

to secure safe-conducts for merchants attending the supervised fairs sponsored by the Counts in the Champagne district. Soon the Champagne fairs became internationally famous as a meeting place where the goods of the north could be exchanged for the products of the south. With the growth of French royal authority under Philip Augustus (1180–1223), safe-conducts became national, and the importance of the fairs was further enhanced as merchants enjoyed the greater security offered by a national administration that assumed the supportive role that had been played formerly, though on a more parochial level, by the Counts of Champagne.

Trade routes multiplied, and contacts were established with all the known world. Gradually, not only France but much of Europe, Russia, the Near East, and North Africa were coursed by trade routes. Merchandise flowed between the Caspian Sea and the Baltic; the Italians connected the Black Sea with the Iberian Peninsula; the goods of Egypt and the farther east flowed across the Mediterranean for transshipment from the Italian ports to all the major cities of Europe. By 1300, as indeed during the previous century, it was possible for the very wealthy to enjoy the assembled luxuries of the world without leaving western Europe. Even so, despite the great distances and the consequent high value per unit of the commodities involved, the trade volume was small, both in bulk and in value, by our standards. On the other hand, the leverage value of even a small volume of trade in stimulating the imagination of a traditional society, in introducing variety into a previously rather bland array of consumption goods, and in generating new habits of mind and new methods of commerce can hardly be underestimated.

THE TOOLS OF TRADE: MEDITERRANEAN DOMINANCE

Confronted by high risks, slow transportation, and long distances, medieval merchants invented—or borrowed, with the readiness that alert businessmen always exhibit when prodded by competition and profit—a versatile range of commercial instruments closely adapted to their needs and environment. For financing overseas ventures and diversifying risks, the *commenda* contract or one of its variants was at once simple and effective. Typically, in the *commenda*, one merchant would contribute two-thirds of the capital while a second would provide the remaining third and, in addition, manage the enterprise abroad, thus justifying his equal share in the profits. In a variant form of the contract, one merchant would put up all the necessary cash and receive three-fourths of the profits, while the second endured the hazards of trading in return for the remaining quarter of the profits. It was thus possible for a young impecunious merchant to trade with the capital of another, more affluent merchant and thereby to accumulate a fund of his own. From the viewpoint of an affluent merchant also, the opportunities afforded by the *commenda* contract were valuable. By negotiating a substantial number of separate contracts, he could assure the safety of his capital through diversification of risks and at the same time enjoy multiple opportunities for profit throughout the commercial world in places so remote that he could not possibly reach them all without utilizing an agent. It is hardly surprising that with everything to gain and with reduced chances of loss, the *commenda* quickly became a very popular device in Mediterranean commerce; its use both between equals and in both directions between the wealthy and the less wealthy is attested in numerous surviving wills and records of Italian merchants. In Genoa, for example, during the fourteenth century, as before, it was not uncommon for a merchant to leave an estate of several, or even a dozen or more, *commenda* contracts at the time of his death.

Particularly in the regions bordering the Mediterranean, a number of other types of credit instruments were developed to meet special needs. Various forms of partnership, in many cases similar to the *commenda*, existed for use in the inland trade, and thus the advantages of diversification of risk and of accumulation of capital present in maritime contracts were transferred to the inland trade. Perhaps the most important of all the trading instruments in making international trade possible was the exchange contract. The movement of goods over long distances involved large enough risks without doubling the hazards through subsequent transshipment of specie in the ultimate settlement of debts and profits. Normally, in international trade, imports and exports tend to balance each other, so that goods exported pay for the goods imported. The importer and the exporter may not, however, always be the same person, so that for each individual transaction payment is required in cash. It was the virtue of the exchange contract to bring together those individuals from one region who, respectively, had credits and debits with regard to another region, so that the debts could cancel the credits without requiring the actual shipment of money. As long as the balance of trade remained roughly even between any two areas, money did not have to be transported for long distances.

As trade became more sophisticated and merchants grew accustomed to the use of credit, the Champagne fairs, strategically placed at the intersection of the active northern and southern trading areas, matured into a financial clearinghouse for the settlement of international debts. Within the framework of the fairs themselves, goods could be bought and sold on credit in anticipation of final settlement at a subsequent fair in one of the other Champagne towns. Perhaps more importantly, however, the regular nature of the fair cycle and the stability of the money of Champagne made it possible for merchants to settle international debts, assumed in other parts of the world, in the money of the fairs, and in the future by means of the exchange contract. Thus a merchant who had money to lend in Constantinople could receive payment from the borrower's agent in France and simultaneously extend credit and avoid the risk of transferring money across the Mediterranean. Metallic money was conserved, dangers were minimized, and the flow of trade was stimulated by the use of the bill of exchange.

Beyond its purely commercial utility, the bill of exchange performed valuable service as a device for bypassing or subverting the clerical proscriptions against usury—the taking of any payment for the lending of money. Excessive attention has probably been devoted to the impact of religious sanctions against usury in limiting economic development during the Middle Ages. The most common form of documentation for the commercial significance of such sanctions is found, after all, in those documents that more or less successfully evaded the intent of the canon law. On the other hand, it is useful to recognize the possibilities inherent in the exchange contract for allowing loans at interest without visible transgression of the law. To this end, a merchant could, since the contract implied that the payment be made in a different place and in a different currency, capitalize upon the variation in exchange rates between two regions so as to conceal the payment of interest. If, for example, a certain number of Genoese pounds were borrowed, and a different number of French *livres tournois* or pounds of Provins were specified for repayment, a subtle knowledge of international exchange rates would be required in order to detect interest hidden in the contract through a favorable exchange rate. Further, it was possible to write such a contract without any intention that the actual repayment would occur in some remote place. Instead, the contract might be liquidated in the very city in which it originated, and thus an ordinary loan could be accomplished under the rubric of the exchange contract, at interest and within one city, without violating, at least on the surface, the religious prohibitions against the taking of interest.

Along the shores of the Mediterranean, then, there existed a highly sophisticated system of finance that could speed the flow of trade, be it domestic or international. By 1300, merchants of the region were well accustomed to credit transactions, and even municipal governments operated on credit, although sometimes forcibly obtained, from the urban population. The great size of many of the Italian cities in relation to the surrounding countryside forced merchants into the broader arena of international competition and, in doing so, sustained and fostered the further growth of the cities. As a consequence of this far-reaching activity, the average level of financial acumen was far greater in the south than in the north of Europe, and despite, or perhaps because of, the dominance of Italian merchants in international commerce, the northern Europeans were slow to adopt the advanced methods that proved so successful in the hands of the southerners.

Throughout most of northwestern Europe at the beginning of our period, transactions were accomplished in silver coin, although by the middle of the fourteenth century, 50 to 100 years after the Italian precedent, gold had become a parallel currency in most countries and was of considerable importance in international trade. Where formal credit instruments were utilized extensively, the commerce was very often between an Italian and a northerner rather than between two northerners. Thus, Italian merchants might advance money to an English wool grower several months before the clip in order to assure a favorable price and a certain supply; similar arrangements developed in the French wine trade and in other commodities throughout Europe wherever the Italians fared. It would be erroneous, however, to suggest that the merchants of northern Europe were totally unaware of the advantages of extending credit themselves or that they were invariably the victims of the Italians; the point is rather one of degree and of technical achievement. Partnerships existed in England and France, just as they did in the south; money was loaned and borrowed in the north, and written records were kept, but never so extensively nor so well as in the south. Often too, in northwestern Europe, many vital occupations in which financial skill was required were dominated by foreign specialists, again most notably the Italians. In France, the royal treasury was first managed by the Order of the Temple, a religious crusading order that could provide both armed security and a trans-Mediterranean complex of chapters that proved invaluable for the international movement of specie. Until 1308, when Philip the Fair, probably seeking an easy means to extinguish his debts and simultaneously to obtain funds, destroyed the Order, the treasury management was shared with a pair of Italians, Ciampolo and Musciatto Franzesi. Again, the heavy special payments levied against the "Lombards," or Italian financiers, in 1311 and 1320 and against the Jews in 1306, 1311, 1315, and 1321 suggests the importance that such foreigners achieved in France in the functioning of internal credit. In England as well, the Italians dominated the financial world. The firms of the Bardi and the Peruzzi were crucial for the provision of royal finance until Edward III defaulted, almost destroying them, in the 1340's. Their place was taken in the fifteenth century by other Italians, including the London branch of the Medici bank. Everywhere, the Italians enjoyed the predominant role in the world of finance, both domestically and internationally, although by the fifteenth century new forces began to appear. Native Englishmen, their coffers swollen with wartime profits, assumed a more active position in England, while France could boast a truly international financier in the person of Jacques Coeur, who provided funds for the court of Charles VII in almost the same measure as Joan of Arc gave spiritual inspiration and who in return very nearly received the same reward, being lucky to escape martyrdom with mere exile. In southern Germany, the slow process of accumulation that was to make the Fugger, the Welser, and the Höchstetter major financial powers in the sixteenth century was already under way.

During the fourteenth and fifteenth centuries, however, a structural dichotomy remained between the southern and northern trading areas of Europe in the matter of financial skill and practice. From the middle of the thirteenth century, the Italians had maintained a truly bimetallic monetary system where gold and silver marched together in the same markets. Only in the fourteenth century did the northerners attempt a gold coinage, and even then it was not really on a par with the silver coinage in domestic transactions, but rather was a supplementary money for use in international trade and diplomatic missions. In the south, the advanced knowledge of credit instruments and the more extensive use of them, tended to economize the metallic currency. Since many international debts could be settled through exchange contracts, and since the widespread employment of the *commenda* lowered the sums that merchants must keep in reserve for safety and for possible profitable opportunities, any given quantity of precious metal gave greater service in the south than in the north. In short, it is very highly probable that the velocity of circulation of precious metal around the shores of the Mediterranean was substantially greater than it was in the north. As a result, the countries of northwestern Europe were more dependent upon their stock of precious metal and more sensitive to variations in its supply.

The Italians consequently had something of an advantage in international trade due to the disparity between the two credit systems. In the south, less money was required for a greater volume of transactions, and therefore capital costs were lower for Italians trading northward than for northerners trading with the south. This in turn tended to affect the north's ability to retain its metallic

reserves, since trade and the profits of trade flowed naturally into
the hands of the better-equipped Italian merchants.

THE GOODS EXCHANGED

Before considering the implications of the disparity between the
northern and southern monetary structures in more detail, it is
necessary to investigate the character of the goods involved in international trade itself. Here again substantial differences existed
between the products of the north and those of the south, and
again this dichotomy is of special significance for an understanding
of the patterns of international trade and of the directions and
nature of monetary movements during the later Middle Ages.

The products of northern trade were typically heavy, bulky commodities of low value per unit; often they were raw or semifinished
materials or food goods. From the fertile plains of Prussian Poland,
grain was exported to feed the cities of Flanders and the Low
Countries. Huge quantities of herring were caught and processed
by Hanseatic fishermen and merchants off the Swedish coast and,
as the fifteenth century progressed, by the Dutch off the coast of
the Netherlands, in the North Sea. Closely related to the fishing
industry was the salt trade. A natural exchange developed between
the Bay of Bourgneuf, on the western coast of France, where the
temperature was high and the skies clear enough to allow the
evaporation of salt, and the northern fishing areas, where the salt
was used to preserve the fish. Along the same routes, wine from
Gascony and La Rochelle traveled northward to England, the Low
Countries, and the towns that formed the Hanseatic trading complex in the Baltic. Many ships were required for the transport of
such heavy goods, and consequently timber for shipbuilding became a strategic item of international commerce. Wood suitable
for shipbuilding was a specialized product in that different types of
timber were specific to different functions within the ship. Oak,
for example, was proper for ribs and keels, but tall, lightweight,
and resilient fir was crucial for masts, spars, and other parts of the
ship's frame. Then too, timber was useless if it lay too far from

water routes, since its great bulk and weight prohibited its economical transportation under the conditions of medieval technology. The shipping industry thus necessitated the tapping of specialized forests accessible to the sea, and consequently considerable commerce developed between the Scandinavian forest areas and the shipbuilding centers of the Low Countries, England, and indeed of all the northern trading community. During the fourteenth century, and especially in the fifteenth, the rapid advancement of military technology—most notably the use of cannon and gunpowder—associated as it was with an increased scale of warfare, placed new strains upon timber supplies and increased the demand for iron of the highest quality. Thus, the need for better armor to withstand first the longbow and then the bullet resulted in increased military consumption of iron and, with iron, of the wood consumed in the forges and furnaces of Europe. Northern iron, particularly Swedish iron, became an important commodity in northern trade.

Perhaps the most valued product of northern Europe and one of the prime balancing items in the trade with the south was raw wool. At the beginning of the fourteenth century, England alone exported close to 40,000 sacks of wool each year to the various cloth-making centers of the world. Large quantities, of course, went to provision the Flemish industry, but the second largest market was almost certainly the collective demand from the cloth towns of Italy. This market, as will soon become apparent, was vitally and strategically significant for the stability of world trade, since wool was the major northern commodity that could be exported in return for the exotic and expensive goods imported from the southern trading region.

Not all the northern commodities were low-cost bulk goods. Indeed, Flemish fine cloth was a luxury of the highest order and found markets throughout the known world—again, as was the case with wool, providing stability and equilibrium in the balance of north–south trade. From the far north—from Russia, Livonia, Poland, and Scandinavia—came exotic furs, such as ermine, sable, and miniver, which garnished the robes of the nobility and the affluent upper bourgeoisie and became one of the foundations of an active trade route running along a north–south axis in

Germany from Nuremberg to Milan, Genoa, and Venice, in addition to serving as a key item in the sea trade from Novgorod to Bruges. Less important, but still significant, a host of miscellaneous goods must be included among the northern products. Amber for jewelry; beeswax for ceremonial candles; honey, a major sweetening agent and for long centuries dominant over sugar; metals such as copper, tin, lead, and even, during the early years of the fourteenth century, sizeable quantities of silver—these could be added to the list of comparatively valuable goods figuring in the trade of the north. Despite the undoubted existence of such products, however, it remains true that in the northern trading region, the typical products were heavy, bulky goods of low value per unit. Certainly the greatest volume of the trade occurred in these items, and they were the goods that occupied the largest number of ships and men.

In the south, the commodities traded were at once more varied and in general more luxurious, but even there a considerable volume of trade occurred in heavy, low-value products. The great cities of Italy, a few major towns in the Islamic world, and Constantinople, perhaps the largest of them all, were incapable, as we already have observed, of feeding themselves from the surrounding countryside. As a result, sea transport of grain from Sicily, the Dalmatian coast, parts of North Africa, and even from the regions bordering the Black Sea became a standard feature of southern commerce. As in the north, the competition for timber grew more intense toward the end of the Middle Ages as local supplies surrounding the older cities were exhausted and it became necessary to seek forests farther afield to find suitable materials for shipbuilding and the great variety of other wood-using activities. During the fourteenth century and particularly in the fifteenth, the rise of the Ottoman Turks and their burgeoning naval strength in the eastern Mediterranean probably increased the demand for the shipbuilding timber that was crucial for the defense of the maritime city-states against this domineering new sea power. The need for reserve fleets meant that more timber must be cut than was actually required for commerce, and at the same time, the fact of naval conflict undoubtedly reduced the service life of ships. Timber, therefore, rose in importance in the southern trading area.

Industrial raw materials played an important part in southern interregional trade as well as in the composition of imports from the north. Wool came not only from England, but also from Spain and North Africa, the domains of the short-stapled Merino sheep. Another major raw material for the cloth industry was alum, the most widely used mordant in the dyeing of cloth and consequently a material with a world-wide market. Alum was derived mainly from mines in Phocaea, on the western coast of Asia Minor, and was a highly profitable Genoese monopoly during the early fourteenth century. Other eastern raw materials included cotton, brought to Europe mainly from the Levant, and silk, which traveled even greater distances, coming as it did from Turkestan and China. Silk, although its trade volume probably remained small throughout the Middle Ages—Lucca, one of the most important producers, imported something over 82 tons of silk annually in the early fourteenth century—must be numbered among the major items of international commerce during the period, chiefly because its value was so great. In the early fifteenth century, for example, one ounce of fine black silk sold in London for the same sum of money that a skilled mason would earn in six full days of labor. Indeed, the very high value of silk even as a raw material, typifies the difference between the trade of the north and that of the south. Whereas northern raw materials consisted of wool, timber, metals, fish, and food grains, the southern primary goods were often light, expensive, and exotic. Ivory from the African coast was exported to France, where a fashion fad during the later Middle Ages favored the use of ivory for combs, delicately carved mirror cases, and decorative inlays of all sorts. Again perhaps, raw materials, but ones of great value, precious stones and jewels were imported in quantity from the Near East. Pearls, rubies, and diamonds enjoyed a brisk market among the wealthiest of northern consumers, while decorative coral from the Levantine coast provided a semiprecious second best for the less affluent or supplemented the collections of the very rich. In some cases, superstitious ends were served, since many of the stones, both precious and semiprecious, were believed to have sacred or magical properties that would protect the wearer from disaster, misfortune, and disease.

Between raw materials and manufactures lay a vast range of

expensive products which were virtually the exclusive preserve of Italian traders. "Spices"—a term that covered everything from pepper and medicinal herbs to dyestuffs and metals—constituted a goodly portion of the monetary worth of any cargo northbound from Italy. The list of such goods is long, numbering in the hundreds, according to one contemporary chronicler, but only a few from the many need here be mentioned. Pepper was one of the most important of the true spices, serving, as it did, to add variety to an otherwise monotonous medieval diet and at the same time to disguise the flavor of food that had passed its peak—probably not a rare occurrence in the long period before modern food preservation techniques. In some years, Venetian pepper imports into western Europe amounted to more than a million pounds. Many other spices, however, supplemented pepper in the long-distance trade. One Venetian galley docking at London in the 1420's, for example, carried ginger, saffron, mace, cinnamon, and rhubarb, the last primarily for medicinal purposes. Even a most incomplete list of the sundry other spices that were shipped all over the medieval world would include sugar from the Levant, cloves, nutmeg, dyestuffs such as indigo, madder, and brazilwood, ambergris, many varieties of nuts, and a host of other exotic products.

Equally important in the trade of the south were finished manufactured goods of great diversity. Interregional trade existed in the coarse woolen cloth and fustian produced in the cloth-making centers of Lombardy, and a similarly active market exchanged the linens and mixed cloths of southern Germany. More typical, however, in the long-distance trade and consequently more significant in structuring over-all trade patterns were the fine luxury products for whose excellence the Mediterranean region rightly became famous. We have already observed the shifts within the Italian textile industry during the fourteenth century that led to increased concentration upon the manufacture of the finest quality woolen cloth and to rapid development of the silk industry throughout the towns of northern Italy. Not only Lucca, but also Venice, Milan, Bologna, Florence, and others, contributed silk products to the flow of international trade. Even more expensive than silk cloth were the cloths of gold and silver, finely interwoven with true threads of precious metal, the heavy damasks and velvets, and the beautiful brocades that were both manufactured in the north of Italy and imported from the east for regional consumption and for transshipment to the north. Specialty manufacturing in the south also contributed accessories to dress, personal jewelry, and many conspicuous decorative ornaments. Bracelets became fashionable in the fourteenth century, and the best of Venetian make were garnished with pearls and diamonds. Venetian pearl buttons were eagerly sought as clothing styles changed from the loose medieval cloak to the tightly buttoned Renaissance doublet and to long gloves with rows of ornamental buttons. Delicately wrought gold buttons from the shops of Cyprus graced purses made from Chinese silk. Fine items of glass and of ivory, silken and velvet bedcoverings, and fine perfumes traveled northward from Italy, and in France in the fifteenth century, one could even find booklatches set with pearls and rubies brought from Alexandria by the Italians. Not all southern manufactures were decorative luxuries for the drawing room, however. From Milan in particular and from parts of southern Germany came the finest weapons and armor in Europe. The skill and craftsmanship required to render plate armor impervious to brutal attack and at the same time sufficiently flexible to permit counterattack kept the price of even the ordinary grades at very high levels. A plain suit of Milanese armor was worth several hundred pounds in the fourteenth century—a sum which at the time could buy as much wheat as we could purchase today for $13,000 or $14,000. The cost of competitive dress, be it the brocades and velvets of the drawing room or the armor of the battlefield, was high and rising during the later Middle Ages. But the cost of failure on the battlefield was greater still; so Milan was assured of an active and growing market at almost any price during the continuous warfare of the fourteenth and fifteenth centuries.

The details of world trade—its merchants' methods and their commodities—could be expanded almost endlessly. Our purpose, however, is to suggest only enough specific sense of the myriad details to give some concreteness to a survey of the broader trends and over-all movements in commerce during the later Middle Ages and to make comprehensible some of the more dramatic dislocations that afflicted trade during our period. In the early years of the fourteenth century, international trade and commerce seemed to be capable of sustaining the rapid rate of growth that it had exhibited since the late twelfth century. Indeed, the so-called commercial revolution was at its peak during those years; but a peak, by definition, is invariably followed by a downturn and a period of contraction. What, then, were the larger patterns of international trade during our period, and what were the sources of change?

STATISTICS OF TRADE

Statistics and quantitative measurements of the volume of international trade, although less rare than for internal trade, remain incomplete, discontinuous, and difficult to interpret, since they often are based upon specific ad valorem taxes and consequently are subject to error attributable to evasion, smuggling, bribery, and special exclusions, to say nothing of the relatively straightforward problem faced by customs officials in determining true value. Despite all such drawbacks, however, we do in fact have more quantitative information regarding the volume of international trade from certain ports and regions than we possess about the levels of almost any other economic activity during the later Middle Ages. Graph VI presents some of the available statistical material concerning medieval international trade.

In order to facilitate comparison among them, the statistics are expressed as a percentage of the maximum trade volume attained during the period covered in each of the four regions. With the two longest series, those of Genoa and Marseille, which extend back into the thirteenth century, it is immediately apparent that the over-all trend is downward throughout the late fourteenth and early fifteenth centuries. The other two series, England and Dieppe, originate only in the fifteenth century; consequently, their peaks necessarily occur somewhat later, but again the trend is downward throughout the greater portion of that century. There is a remarkable degree of congruency among all four trend lines during the first 65 years of the fifteenth century, when all move precipitously downwards, reaching their nadir in the fourteen-sixties. For these trading areas, it seems difficult to doubt that the fifteenth century was anything but a period of economic recession. Some scholars

GRAPH VI International Trade, 1270–1550 (Expressed as a Percentage of the Area Maximum During the Time Span for Which Statistics Were Available)

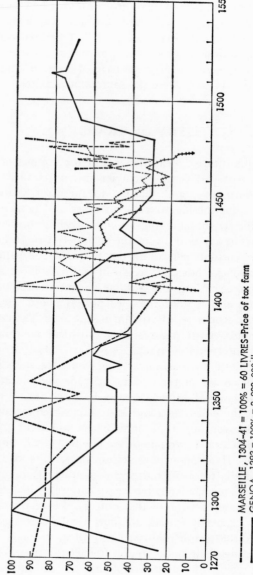

------- MARSEILLE, 1304-41 = 100% = 60 LIVRES–Price of tax farm
—·—·— GENOA, 1293 = 100% = 3,822,000 lb
– – – ENGLAND, 1405-8 = 100% = 187,439£
+++++++ DIEPPE, 1424-5 = 100% = 390 SHIPS granted permission to enter or depart

SOURCES: M. M. Postan, "The Trade of Medieval Europe: the North," *op. cit.*, for England; H. Sieveking, "Aus Genueser Rechungs- und Steuerbüchern," *Sitzungsberichte der Kais. Akad. der Wissenschaften in Wien*, Vienna, 1909, for Genoa; E. Baratier and F. Reynaud, *Histoire du commerce de Marseille*, for Marseille; M. Mollat, *Le commerce maritime Normand à la fin du Moyen Age*, Librairie Plon, Paris, 1952, for Dieppe.

have argued that since the European population declined following the plagues of the latter half of the fourteenth century, the per capita volume of international trade may have remained constant. It is apparent from Graph VI, however, that the trade figures in all cases in 1460 were less than 40 per cent of their peak levels, but no scholar has argued that the population decline exceeded 30 or 40 per cent of the total. It is, therefore, certain that the per capita volume of international trade declined severely in all four of these regions.

Now, the performance of four regions is not equivalent to an index of the total volume of world trade. Other ports could have arisen, and shifts could have occurred in the old trade routes. Yet it hardly seems likely that three major ports and an entire country could experience such a sharp recession without their affecting markets elsewhere. International trade, after all, is, by definition, interconnection; inevitably any one country's troubles tend to be transmitted very quickly to all the others within the trading area. Further, there survives a mass of nonquantitative evidence regarding other European ports—enough to suggest that trade elsewhere also suffered a period of decline during the later Middle Ages. An ordinance of Charles V of France in May, 1376, for example, seeks to alleviate the hardship caused by the collapse of trade in the port of Harfleur. To the north, the merchants from the Hanseatic towns found commerce increasingly disturbed by war and political turmoil during the fifteenth century, and as that century progressed, trade and profits appear to have declined at an accelerating rate. To some extent, Dutch and English competition may have contributed to the slump, but at least until the last decades of the fifteenth century, it was more intense competition for a smaller total volume of trade. It appears probable, then, that throughout western Europe, the aggregate volume of trade was declining during the later Middle Ages; but again, not all ports and not all commodities suffered equally. More complex still, and therefore more fascinating as an historical problem, is the fact that the sequence of events—the timing of the difficulties—was not the same everywhere nor even among different products within the same region.

CRISIS

For purposes of analysis, we may profitably divide the factors affecting trade into three broad classes: external political circumstance; technology, as it altered transport and shipping skills; and finally, the totality of the more or less economic variables that influenced markets and production. From the very beginning of our period, the pressure of political circumstance had a profound effect upon patterns of commerce. In the early fourteenth century, the Flemish were at war with the French, and as a result, the financial needs of the French king rose at the same time as the Flemish merchants forfeited their ability to travel safely through his kingdom. Fiscal problems deriving from the costs of war led Philip the Fair to seek additional sources of revenue, first by imposing a sales tax on the goods exchanged at the Champagne fairs and then, considerably more disruptively, seizing goods and accounts receivable from the Jews and the Lombards mentioned above. Now, the chief factor in the growth of the fairs had been the security they offered for the exchange of northern goods for southern and, as the thirteenth century progressed, for the international clearing of commercial credits and debits. From the early fourteenth century, the fairs were deprived of these special advantages. If the Flemish could no longer attend, the fairs were less profitable for the Italians; if confiscatory taxes and levies could arbitrarily strip merchants and moneylenders of their capital, then the value of the fairs as an international clearing house was negligible. Under such circumstances, the relatively minor sales tax was only an additional burden and surely not the cause of the fairs' difficulties. It did, however, push in the same direction as the other burdens, and all taken together account for the rapid decline of the Champagne fairs after the beginning of the fourteenth century.

Alternatives, both by land and by sea, that could more efficiently serve the needs of international trade were soon sought. Shipping technology had improved, so that sail power increasingly displaced manual labor in both northern and southern waters. In the north, rudders were shifted from the gunwales to the sternpost, and sails became increasingly maneuverable during the course of the thirteenth and fourteenth centuries, producing a more seaworthy and less labor-consuming ship. In the Mediterranean, marine charts grew more accurate as navigators recorded and refined their empirical observations, and sails slowly supplemented oars even on the galleys. Thus, perhaps under the stimulus of the difficulties in France, merchants from both the north and the south utilized such technological achievements to extend the range of their trading activities. In the latter half of the fourteenth century, Hanseatic merchants appeared in force among the salt buyers along the Gascon coast, and by the fifteenth century, they had established a colony in Lisbon. Somewhat earlier, the Italians began to bypass the old land route through central France; they developed the sea lanes through the Straits of Gibraltar and along the Atlantic coast of Europe to Bruges, London, and Southampton, where markets were already in session and where permanent agents could handle transactions at the termini of the new trade routes. On land also, rather than risk the dangers of central France, merchants shifted their routes to the east; during the fifteenth century, Geneva replaced Champagne as the site of the most prominent international fairs. It remained so until Louis XI (1461–83) was able to direct the rising national power of France into a concerted effort to destroy the Geneva fairs and to relocate the major center at Lyons.

Political circumstance must surely be accorded the dominant role in the decline of the Champagne fairs and in the relocation of the European overland trade routes. The same is true of other areas and other routes throughout the course of the later Middle Ages. We have already noted the disruption of the Flemish woolen industry that occurred when the French and the English, at war with one another, were constricting both food and wool supplies in the endeavor to use economic weapons to force the Flemish to ally with one side or the other. The effects of the Hundred Years' War upon trade were more widespread, however; deployment of hostile naval forces altered long-established commercial practices and trade routes elsewhere as well. The English-held portions of France, centering around the vineyards of Bordeaux and Gascony, were the primary source of supply for the northern wine trade. Although Anglo-French conflict in the twenties had already distressed this commerce, the out-

break of the Hundred Years' War was a veritable catastrophe, reducing wine exports by three-fourths in the single year 1337. From
then on, English and Gascon ships were compelled to sail in convoy
in order to protect their cargoes of wine from French predators—
a fairly successful effort, but one that increased the costs of wine
shipments more than threefold. Wine prices consequently rose
abruptly in the late thirteen-thirties and remained high until the
Black Death, in 1348–49. Thereafter, under the combined pressure
of labor scarcity, war, the destruction of vineyards, and a partial
French reconquest of the Bordeaux region, wine prices in England
were roughly double their early fourteenth-century levels.

The multitude of political events buffeting medieval world trade
obviously cannot be adequately accounted for here; such a study
would require a history of the entire world and scrutiny in detail
of every distant corner and terminus of international commerce.
The Turks' steady conquest of territories bordering the eastern
Mediterranean changed the balance of commercial power in that
region; the debut of the Ming dynasty in 1368 brought to an end
the period of security for Asian travelers and made it more difficult
to procure silk. Changes in North African politics affected gold
flows, interurban power struggles restructured the economic centers of Italy, and anti-Italian sentiment throughout the north dictated the choice of ports as strongly as did economic considerations.
Such factors, crucial though they were, must be treated only inad-
equately here; we shall attempt to cover only the most prominent
determinants of international trade patterns and, where possible,
we shall call attention to some of the external political forces
which inhibited and complicated the free exchange of goods.

DEATH AND DISPLAY

The most far-reaching event of the later Middle Ages was beyond doubt the plague of 1348–49, reinforced in its effects by its
subsequent recurrences; we have traced its impact on agriculture
and on the urban economy. We must now consider it again in the
context of international trade. Before so doing, let us briefly re-
order some of the fragments of our previous analysis. In the agri-

cultural sectors of almost all of the countries of western Europe, a series of adjustments were made by producers in response to the plague, in order to shift assets into areas where demand remained higher than that for the basic food grains, but with a few exceptions, mainly in northern Italy, these strategic shifts had failed to maintain agricultural revenues at high levels. Taxes and, in some areas, wartime destruction further acted to weaken the rural economy and to siphon funds from the countryside into the cities. The rise of manufactured prices in relation to agricultural prices greatly extended this imbalance. In the towns, the primary and immediate consequence of the plague was probably an increase in per capita wealth and, by the same token, in the enhanced demand for luxury products, partially met by an upgrading of diet but more dramatically visible in changes of taste favoring the conspicuous consumption of expensive items of personal adornment. Thus, among textiles, the silk industry flourished, while sales of coarser grades of wool tended to suffer.

Now, the increasing taste for luxury products within the towns—indeed throughout entire states—was virtually a Pan-European phenomenon and one with multitudinous economic ramifications. Italy, as always, presents a somewhat distinct case since she was in essence the fashion leader of the world and the model for luxurious style. Even in Italy, however, the inheritance effects of the plague widened and deepened the consumption of luxury goods. Elsewhere, particularly throughout northern Europe, temporary affluence in conjunction with the fear of imminent death greatly forwarded the imitation and assimilation of Italian fashion, fabrics, and ornaments. The ordinary visitor walking through the medieval collection in the Louvre in Paris can almost invariably distinguish those paintings made after the initial plague of the fourteenth century simply by observing the style of the clothing. Historians of costume record the later fourteenth century as a period in which every possible attention was given to personal adornment without regard to the expense. Geoffrey Chaucer, poet, controller of customs on wool, wine, and hides in the Port of London, and favorite at the court of Richard II, in his *Parson's Tale* makes the Parson bewail, in traditional fashion, his contemporaries' "sinful costly array of clothing and namely in too much superfluity or else in too disordinate scantiness." The age-old complaint, however, becomes specific to the fourteenth century when it denounces the "cost of embroidering" and "other waste of cloth in vanity" and the "excess of furring in their gowns." Perhaps more substantial, if more banal, evidence of the taste for luxury may be found in the numerous sumptuary laws of France and England that followed upon the plague; the first such English act was passed in 1363 as the result of a Parliamentary petition of the preceding year.

If the terror of the plague served to increase the desire for superfluous display and outward signs of well-being and wealth, its mortality sharply curtailed the capacity of most nations to satisfy those desires; it was no longer possible to produce those fine products in the quantity demanded. Everywhere, the labor supply was reduced, and as we have seen, it is quite probable that skilled labor suffered most severely, since the training and replacement period was necessarily longer in that category. The taste for personal decoration only exacerbated this difficulty since one of the distinctive traits of luxury products is the care expended in their manufacture, which in turn implies greater quantities of embodied labor—more precisely, skilled labor, the very input which was most scarce after the pestilence. Misallocation of a scarce resource in a period of economic turbulence obviously weakens any economy, even one closed and insulated from international problems. No European country in the later Middles Ages was so insulated, however, and consequently the allocation of labor affected the international balance of payments as well as the domestic economies of the separate states.

Since skilled labor was scarce and no substitute existed, and since the demand for luxury was high, it seems to have been physically impossible in many countries to supply the demand for such goods through domestic production alone. In addition to this, many of the most desired products were not indigenous to northwestern Europe; silks, brocades, many precious stones, perfume, and a host of spices were available only from the south, while amber and the best furs came from eastern Europe beyond the Elbe. Taken together, these factors put considerable pressure upon the balance of payments of many countries in northern Europe; but they were not in themselves sufficiently powerful to cause persistent outflows of precious metals. Imports are but half of the equation, and it is necessary therefore to consider now the level of exports that under normal circumstances serve to balance the cost of imports. Here we may again recall the nature of the goods that were typical of northern commerce—heavy, low-value food products, metals, timber, and fish. Some exceptions existed in the amber and fine furs of the northeast, which will be considered shortly, and in the finest woolen cloths from the Low Countries and, by the second half of the fourteenth century, from England, but the ordinary product exchanged in the north was heavy, relatively inexpensive, and not commercially successful in a luxury-oriented world.

In fact, the commodities of northern commerce were precisely those which were likely to be most severely hurt by the aftermath of the plagues, since they depended most heavily upon the existence of a broad market. Disease sharply diminished the number of consumers and at the same time raised both the quantity and quality of land per capita among the survivors, so as further to reduce demand for food grains and to increase the competition among the suppliers of such alternative products as wool. The very nature of the commodities of northern trade made them intrinsically more vulnerable to the economic consequences of the plagues; but this was not all. The growing domestic demand for luxury goods in such countries as France and England meant that a substantial portion of the domestic skilled labor force was drawn into the production of such goods for home consumption. Even after the fine brocades, silks, and velvets had been imported from the south, they had then to be made into clothing and tailored to fit. Changes in style, for example the substitution of the closely tailored Renaissance doublet for the loose medieval cloak or of the exotic rolled, peaked, and jeweled hats of Italian origin for the traditional hood, raised the level of labor input per garment. Pressure was thus put on domestic labor resources, and to the extent that labor was pulled toward the production of such finery for home consumption, it was withdrawn or pre-empted from the manufacture of exportable goods that might have competed for the luxury markets of the world. From several sides—the increase in imports, the decrease in exports, the misallocation of scarce labor resources—economic con-

creasingly unfavorable for northwestern Europe, and the terms
of trade appear to have shifted in favor of the south. There is
every indication that the period was marked by substantial and
fairly constant losses of precious metal, both gold and silver, and
further, that this metal flowed toward the Mediterranean region—
the emporium of splendor and personal magnificence.

One other region, northeastern Europe, seems to have benefited
from the shift in the terms of trade. The Hanse towns along the
Baltic coast were the primary northern source of fur, wax, and
amber—three commodities for which per capita demand probably
rose after the plagues. Fur of the best grades—sable at 82 ducats,
marten at 30 ducats, and ermine at 14 ducats per hundred skins
during the reign of Henry IV of England—vied with the silks of
the south as outward signs of affluence. In the single year 1405,
450,000 pieces of fur were shipped from Riga, on the Baltic, to
Bruges, where presumably they found a brisk market; and Riga
was not the only source of supply. The same ships carried a quantity of wax worth almost half as much as the furs and destined for
ceremonial use throughout the churches of the northwest. Here
again it seems likely that the increased death rate of the period
caused an increase in the demand for candles made from the beeswax required for religious use; one of the most frequent legacies
to the church in this period was an endowment for the perpetual
purchase of candles for the benefit of the soul of the donor. Testaments of the members of the London bourgeoisie who died during
the late fourteenth and fifteenth centuries rarely neglected to make
provision for the purchase of candles. Taken together, then, the
per capita demand for northeastern amber, furs, and wax probably
grew after the initial visitation of the Black Death, and so, in
virtually direct proportion, did the pressure on the bullion supplies
of northwestern Europe.

THE BALANCE OF PAYMENTS

Italians and Hansards

Economic conditions certainly tended to produce a drain of
precious metals from northwestern Europe, but unfortunately, no

direct statistical evidence allows us to know its magnitude. Two
bodies of indirect evidence, however, confirm the severity of the
problem. On the one hand, there is the almost universal contemporary outcry regarding the loss of bullion and the consequent
inadequacy of the domestic money supplies of the nations concerned and, on the other, there are the extant coinage figures from
several northern countries. England, as always, provides the best
evidence, since her coinage figures have been preserved intact. It
is also helpful that we know that a very large proportion—90 per
cent or more between 1304 and 1325—of her coinage output was
struck from resmelted foreign coin. Clearly, then, the level of
English mint production was closely related to the balance of payments, so that when the balance was favorable, the mints tended to
be active and vice versa. Graph VII shows the level of silver coinage
in England over the 200-year span 1270–1470.

It is immediately apparent from Graph VII that the levels of
mint production suffered a very pronounced slump after the
decade of the thirteen-fifties. Indeed, if one compares the active
years from 1273 to 1322 with the hundred-year period 1363–1464,
the level of coinage in the latter period averages only 3.8 per cent
of that attained in the earlier period. The English silver coinage
figures surely confirm our proposition that the balance of payments
was not favorable to northwestern Europe, and these statistics do
not stand alone. In the case of gold as well, mint outputs declined
more or less steadily after the first burst of activity in the twenty
years following the initiation of the gold coinage in 1344. Production between 1363 and 1464 averaged only 28 per cent of that between 1344 and 1363; after a brief but not insignificant recovery
in the early fifteenth century, outputs retreated even more sharply
and remained a mere trickle until well into the fourteen-sixties.
Elsewhere in northwestern Europe, the same phenomenon recurs. In
France, gold coinage levels in the latter half of the fourteenth century were less than a third of the mid-century average and less than
one-eighth of that for the peak year 1339. In the case of silver, the
decline, as in England, was more severe still. Before 1360, annual
silver outputs of over 100,000 marks were not uncommon; thereafter, coinage did not exceed 30,000 marks until the end of the
century, and the average ran closer to 4,000 or 5,000 marks. Such

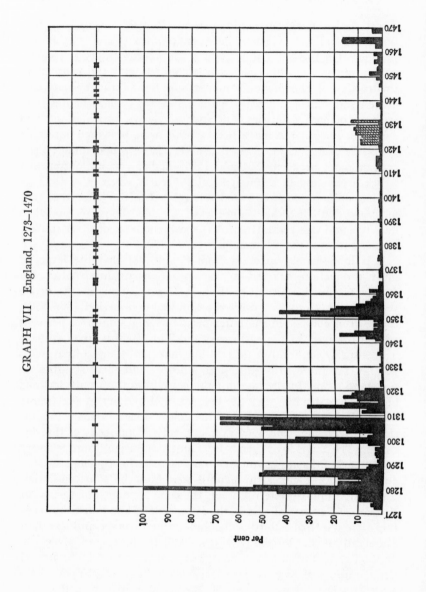

GRAPH VII England, 1273–1470

figures as we have for Flanders confirm the same pattern of decline.

Throughout the northwest, then, coinage levels fell, and they did so despite the concerted efforts of rulers to raise them. Monetary historians have described the period of a "war of monies" in which princes adjusted exchange rates, passed severe laws requiring holders of bullion to bring it to the mint, and attempted to force patterns of international trade so as to shift the balance of payments in their own favor. All of these efforts failed, but the strength of the attempts and the high level of political concern with the problem render it even more likely that coinage figures are in fact fairly accurate measures of the state of the international balance of payments. Further, as a result of this interest, a number of inquiries were made to discover the causes of the metal shortage, and consequently we have a substantial body of contemporary opinion regarding the factors believed to influence the balance. In Graph VII, I have plotted the dates of ordinances and parliamentary petitions decrying the scarcity of coin and the export of money. The quantity of complaint is clearly correlated with the actual scarcity of coin, since the greatest concentration of petitions lies in areas of very low mint output. The surviving comments, then, are not merely the random views of simple men longing for more ready money, but rather the informed judgments of those who knew the facts and were in a position to analyze the problem.

What did these men see as the cause of the great shortage of bullion and coined money? Merchants and experts of the period were sophisticated enough to avoid overly simplified arguments, and consequently their explanations were multi-faceted. The aspect that presently concerns us is the contemporary assertion of the direct connection between monetary flows and the balance of trade—that is, monetary loss directly due to commerce and not to political,

GRAPH VII

Total silver coinage in pounds Tower expressed as a percentage of the output of the year 1280 with the dates of ordinances and petitions regarding the export or scarcity of coin shown above. Coinage of Calais is indicated by diagonal lines.

SOURCES: Sir John Craig, *The Mint*; C. G. Crump and C. Johnson, "Tables of Bullion Coined under Edward I, II, III"; R. Ruding, *Annals of the Coinage*.

military, or other such expenditures. In England in 1378–79, Parliament requested import prohibitions against cloth of gold, silk, handkerchiefs, precious stones, jewels, and furs. In 1381, one Richard Leyc stated that precious metal was exported because of the excessive consumption of "grocery, mercery, furs, ivory, etc." Also in the same vein was a series of regulations that sought to limit exports of wool unless a portion of the sale price was returned to England in cash and to force foreign merchants to purchase as many English wares as would equal the value of the foreign goods that they had sold. The villains among the foreign merchants were almost invariably the Italians; in 1409, an ordinance was passed prohibiting the smuggling of precious metal from the country by concealing it in shipments of goods. Presumably the Italians were the intended target, since the reality of this practice can be documented, with regard to the city of Bruges, in the Medici archives for the early fifteenth century. The Venetians are specifically accused, in a document of 1404, of importing false coin, and "Lombards," meaning all Italians, are denounced for employing "letters of Lombard" and other devious means to export coin from the realm. The "letter of Lombard" was undoubtedly an exchange contract; in this case, the competitive advantage which accrued to the Italians as a result of their superior financial technique was directly blamed for some of the difficulties of the English. Again, and for the same reasons, the Italians appear as evildoers in a long and curious propagandistic poem on English trade, *The Libelle of Englyshe Polycye,* written about 1436. Its burden is that too many fripperies were imported and that the Italians gained too much profit from their manipulation of exchange contracts. Contemporaries clearly felt that there was in fact a bullion drain, that it was at least in part the result of an adverse balance of trade, and that the purveyors of luxury goods, most notably the Italians, were responsible for much of the trouble.

We have distinguished between northeastern and northwestern Europe on the basis of the commodities offered in trade: public opinion in the later Middle Ages was not silent in this regard and condemned the northeastern luxuries as well as the southern. The excessive use of fur was perhaps the most common complaint, but it must be granted that criticism of the German traders was somewhat muted compared to the wholesale denunciation of the Italians. To a certain extent, this may be explained by the success of English merchants in invading the Hanse preserves along the Baltic. In the half-century between 1339, when Edward III had been driven to pawn his and the Queen's crowns at Trèves and Cologne, and 1385, when an English fleet could challenge the Germans off the coast of the Zwin, much progress had been made. By 1388, the English had established a trading station in Danzig and were increasingly competitive in the north. Despite this, however, the Hansards did come in for a good measure of criticism for exporting money through the import of fur, and we know from occasional cargo lists that the quantities involved were very large. It seems safe, therefore, to assume that money flowed from the northwest to the northeast, but there is surprisingly little contemporary comment about abundance of money in the Hanseatic trading regions. Indeed, there appears to have been a monetary shortage there of almost the same dimensions as that which prevailed in France and England following the plagues. Significantly, however, evidence from the Hanse towns does reveal a greatly increased propensity for luxury consumption, and it is perhaps this factor, combined with weaker grain markets, that balanced the inflow of specie seeking the northern goods of butter, fur, wax, and amber against a greatly expanded outlay for the Mediterranean luxuries carried over the north–south overland trade route—a commerce historically documented, if statistically obscure. As a result of this commerce and the new incursions by sea, Hanseatic merchants became extremely distrustful of the Italians during the later Middle Ages and, at the Diet of Lunebourg in 1412, even went so far as to prohibit any further commercial activity by Italians in the north. Every effort was made to restrict the privileges of the Hanse to long-term residents of the Hanse towns, and thus, by the same token, to exclude both the English and the ubiquitously despised Italians. Despite all attempts at limitation, however, the amount of commercial interaction between the Hanse towns and the Nuremberg-Frankfurt-Mediterranean trading complex increased during the course of the fourteenth and early fifteenth centuries. Equally serious was the growth of the east–west land route through Nuremberg, which paralleled the traditional Hanseatic sea route and thus provided overland competition for the most highly priced and desirable goods. The east–west route simultaneously undermined the Hanseatic monopoly in northern luxuries and enhanced the economic position and importance of Nuremberg as a major junction on the north–south land route, but in terms of bullion movements, it was the north–south route itself that caused the greatest problems for the Hanse. In 1405, the merchants of Lübeck, one of the most important Hanse towns, lashed out directly at the merchants of Nuremberg, declaring that "they sell all kind of articles . . . thread and silk, articles from Frankfurt as well as Venice . . . they also sell pearls and gold by the ounce . . . they sell more in one day than your merchants and bourgeois in a year." [1] The continental termini of this overland trading route were Milan, Genoa, and Venice. With all deference to possible exaggeration on the part of self-serving merchants resentful of competition, it would seem that there was an active and probably one-sided trade that connected the northern and southern economies and drew precious metals toward the south. Consequently, money that had initially flowed from northwest to northeast did not accumulate in the latter region because of the simultaneous southward flow of funds in search of Mediterranean luxury goods.

The Coffers of Rome

Before attempting to trace the course of monetary movements in the Mediterranean areas, it is necessary to recognize, as did the experts of the time, that the causes of the drain on the metal resources of the north were more complicated than a mere dislocation of the commercial balance of payments. Equally strident voices were raised against the Church, condemning its role in draining funds from northern Europe, indeed from all of Christendom. We have already observed that one of the results of the tremendously increased death rate in the latter half of the fourteenth century was an increase in the legacies to the Church, which sustained the purchase of such commodities as silk for vestments and wax for candles—items that affected the commercial balance of payments. This

[1] Quoted in P. Dollinger, *La Hanse, xiie–xviie siècles* (Paris: Aubier, 1964), p. 513.

was not all, however; the Church also accumulated large sums of unrestricted cash both through donations from the living, who hoped to avert misfortune, and from the estates of the dead, who had sought to be spared in the afterworld from some of the pains of their sins. Equally too, the Church, as a major landholder everywhere in Europe, collected immense death duties and entry fines, which were a direct function of human mortality, and in this sense benefited from the public suffering, at least in the early stages of the age of pestilence. Thereafter, it will be recalled, the Church shared the problems common to all great landowners—shortage of labor, rising costs, and declining produce prices—but since the revenue sources of the Church were multiple, she was to some extent insulated from the economic problems of ordinary feudal lords. In the short run, then, economic circumstance worked wholly to concentrate funds in the coffers of the Church, and in the long run, after the initial benefits of a more rapid rural death rate had dissipated and the net effect of the plagues had become decidedly negative in the agricultural sector, the Church still accumulated funds through its nonagricultural activities. These funds could be, and were, sent first to Rome, then, during the period of the Babylonian Captivity, to Avignon, and finally, when the Schism produced two rival popes, the revenues were divided between Rome and Avignon, depending upon the allegiance of the paying country. With the resolution of the Schism and the election of Martin V in 1417, the papacy and the revenues returned to Rome.

Acting as they did to worsen the already severe shortage of money and, in addition, during the Avignon period, subject to the criticism that they were used for political purposes by the French, papal transfers and remittances were enormously unpopular. In 1366, Edward III of England prohibited the collection of Peter's Pence, a papal revenue originally levied as a penny from every Christian, and he simultaneously banned the transfer of such revenues overseas. In 1381, at a monetary conference in London, one John Hoo recommended that the papal collector be an Englishman and, further, that papal revenues be transferred only in the form of English goods, so as to economize on scarce specie. Similar examples of covetous national concern with papal remittances recur in England in 1376, 1384, 1399, 1409, and 1433. In France, the popular clamor was comparable despite the fact that the papacy was temporarily located in Avignon; it became louder during the fifteenth century, with the resolution of the Schism and the return of the papacy to Rome. In 1461, the Parlement of Paris made a direct and itemized evaluation of the losses of bullion caused by the Church and judged that they averaged 300,000 *écus* per year. For this reason, the Parlement petitioned the King not to abrogate the Pragmatic Sanction, the royal decree of 1438 that freed the French Church from papal taxation and gave the King considerable control over ecclesiastical matters. In the opinion of the members of the Parlement, abrogation of the decree would have raised the papal take to 2,800,000 *écus* annually.

Where we have records, it would seem that such concern was justified. The sums taken by the papacy were in fact very substantial, but more important, these transfers, often in specie, occurred in the absence of any counterbalancing item to return the lost metal to the bullion-starved north. For France, where the figures have been studied in detail by Jean Favier through the records of the Avignon papacy, it appears that the average remittances from France to Avignon between 1378 and 1398 ran close to 700 marks of gold per year.[2] The significance of such a drain can be properly comprehended when it is further recognized that this sum represented more than one-third of the total annual gold coinage of France during the same period. The leverage exercised by such a drain on the money supply of a country without gold mines must have been immense. Unfortunately, we are not so well informed regarding the revenues of the Roman papacy, but what evidence there is suggests that that body took roughly equal revenues from those parts of the world which rendered allegiance to Rome. If this is true, then the English surely had as just a cause for complaint against Rome as the French had against Avignon. To the south, the Iberian Peninsula, which favored Avignon, became an increasingly important source of papal revenue as the fifteenth century progressed, and indeed surpassed even France after 1404. By 1454–

---

[2] Jean Favier, *Les Finances pontificales a l'époque du grand schisme d'Occident, 1378–1409* (Paris: Éditions E. de Boccard, 1966). The comparison to the total gold coinage of France is based on my own *Money, Prices, and Foreign Exchange in Fourteenth Century France* (New Haven: Yale University Press, 1963).

58, the papal tenth in Spain was reportedly 2,000,000 marks, and the period was referred to as the "evacuación de oro"—the flight of gold. While it is perhaps prudent to take the actual figure with a certain amount of caution in the Spanish case, there can be little doubt that the papal collectors there, as elsewhere in Europe, contributed greatly to the problem of monetary scarcity.

Diplomacy

To the two foregoing causes of monetary scarcity—the adverse balance of trade between the north and the south and the loss of specie to the Church—it is necessary to add another, namely, losses of bullion as a result of military and diplomatic expense. We have already included the cost of armor and weapons from Milan and southern Germany under the rubric of commercial balances, and we have observed that the expenditures for such goods were kept at boom levels by the endless wars of the fourteenth and fifteenth centuries. Military expenditures, however, were made not only for personal equipment, but also for mercenaries and mercenary fleets. The introduction by the English of the longbow and its spectacular success in the Hundred Years' War forced the French to seek a countervailing power to neutralize the devastating effect of rapid-fire archery. The available soldiers were found in the south; in one battle, 6,000 trained Genoese crossbowmen were employed, and throughout the entire war, the French kings depended more heavily upon mercenary forces than had been the custom among their predecessors in the days before the feudal knight was becoming manifestly obsolete. In naval warfare as well, the Italians, long the masters of ocean trading in the Mediterranean, offered the most readily available fleets, composed of the most efficient fighting ships of the period. Consequently, both sides in the Anglo-French war expended very substantial sums for the services of Italian fleets, and a number of enterprising Italians found their fortunes by acting as agents between northern monarchs and southern cities capable of mustering sea power rapidly. Needless to say, since the expenditures of one side forced like escalation of expenditures by the other, the market remained both active and a costly drain of precious metals, once more in the direction of the Mediterranean. The scale of such naval outlays could be immense; at the turn of the thirteenth century, the French spent over 1½ million *livres tournois* for this purpose alone. Closely related to military costs were expenditures for diplomacy—the making of allies or the endeavor to subvert or neutralize potential enemies. The amounts spent for such purposes cannot be detailed, but there is no doubt that they were substantial and recurrent. Money flowed from England to Flanders, to Holland, and to Bavaria at various times during the course of the war; it passed from France to the Kingdom of Castile, to Savoy, and, during the final phase of the war, to Burgundy; but this is at best no more than a skeletal outline. Two primary economic consequences resulted from these expenditures. In the first place, when attempts were made to win allies to the south, the necessary payments reinforced the already serious drain in that direction. In the second, by removing money from domestic hoards and creating windfall profits for foreign princes, diplomatic expenditures probably increased the velocity of circulation and raised the demand for luxury products among the recipients, and this in turn probably directed additional funds toward the southern suppliers of such goods.

Under the triple pressure of shifts in consumption patterns, of papal remittances, and of military and diplomatic expenditures, the northern regions of Europe tended to lose precious metals. The economic consequences of this continuous drain were ultimately severe. After the initial incursion of the Black Death, there was a notable reduction in economic activity throughout Europe which, in the opinion of many historians and most contemporaries, was serious enough to merit the term "depression." On the other hand, some historians—I am not among them—have judged that the increase in per capita wealth outweighed the total decline and have found the period one if not of progress, of regeneration, in which the potential for future growth was created. This latter view, although it is ultimately justified by the fact that growth did indeed resume in the sixteenth century, neglects, in my opinion, a necessary middle stage. That stage was a secondary period of recession brought about by the exhaustion of the bullion supplies, and thus of the effective purchasing power of the populations of northern Europe. As bullion losses consistently exceeded increments to the coinage, and in the absence, especially in the north, of any adequate money substitutes, economic activity slowed even further than it had in the immediate wake of the plague. At that point, however, the laws of classical economics began to operate, and there was a tendency to return to equilibrium—a tendency reinforced, as we shall see, by concerted state action to reverse the outflows of bullion. During the fifteenth century, population began to recover, slowly at first and then, toward the end of the period, rapidly. The market for agricultural goods was thus gradually restored, the relative position of the rural sector improved, and a growing share of the consumer's budget was directed toward domestic food purchases. At the same time, the continued loss of specie began to limit the effective demand for luxury goods, and the purveyors of southern luxuries found it more and more difficult to receive payment for their goods. Graph VI (p. 130) indicates the progressive decline in trade volume during the first half of the fifteenth century, and it would seem fairly certain, given the complaints of a number of Italian merchants at this time, that the decline was at least in some considerable part the result of the inability of northern consumers to pay for their goods, either in commodities useful to the south or in cash. Partly too, it was caused by the unwillingness of northern princes to condone further losses of bullion.

Throughout northern Europe, efforts were made to attack the problem of bullion loss at its source. Sumptuary legislation, government control of standards of fashion and table, had been known in some European countries for centuries, but its primary purposes had been religious and social—to prevent sinful ostentation and pride of dress, or to maintain important class distinctions and support the social hierarchy. Such, for example, appears to have been the case with the thirteenth-century Spanish sumptuary laws. In the later fourteenth century, however, sumptuary legislation became more urgent and extensive, and its purpose was often explicitly related to the commercial balance of trade. The English sumptuary act of 1363 follows directly upon a Parliamentary petition of the preceding year demanding limitation of consumption before the "wealth of the kingdom is destroyed." Even more forceful are direct prohibitions against the export of money, which appear in English legislation in 1348, 1351, 1364, 1409, 1439, and 1449. In

1365, the English governor of Ponthieu was ordered to search travelers to see if they were exporting coin, and actual prosecution for this crime is recorded in 1371. Comparable legislation, both sumptuary laws and the direct prohibition of the export of coin, were reiterated in France. One of the charges brought against Jacques Coeur, the great mid-fifteenth century French financier, was based on his role in impoverishing the realm through the export of silver. In France also, there was an attempt to substitute domestic manufactures for imported luxuries. The frequently cited edict of Louis XI in 1466, establishing the French silk industry, explicitly connects the outflow of massive quantities of gold with the importation of silk hosiery from the south. We have already noted some of the Hanseatic restrictions against Italian traders and have observed that their origin lay, at least in part, in a concern for the balance of payments. By the end of the fourteenth century, Flanders and Burgundy had instituted monetary restrictions, and even on the Iberian Peninsula, monetary export was either forbidden or closely regulated. Throughout northern Europe, then, there were by the middle of the fifteenth century a number of influences, both economic and political, working in concert to slow the outflow of precious metals toward the south. Losses could not continue indefinitely without exhausting bullion supplies; population growth had begun to reverse the imbalance between the rural and the urban sectors of the northern economies; and finally, the rising power of northern monarchs in the late fifteenth century increased the political force behind those edicts and measures designed to quell the outflow of bullion. Though the outflows never entirely ceased, new mining technology from Germany and ultimately the discovery of vast new mines in the Americas almost totally eliminated the problem of bullion scarcity by flooding Europe with growing amounts of precious metal after about 1460.

THE MEDITERRANEAN SOUTH

If northern Europe suffered losses of bullion, who gained? In the initial phase of the monetary movement, it was, of course, the people of the Mediterranean regions, particularly the Italians. Since they had long since established themselves as the western world's best and most strategically placed financiers, the Italians could and did reap immense profits from the international transfer of money. Since such transfers were a dominant factor in the economics of the period, a number of Italian bankers found both profit and power despite the widespread economic contraction that afflicted many sections of the world economy. Such advantages did not, however, arise without risk. In 1343, the great banking house of the Peruzzi fell, and three years later it was followed into ruin by the even greater firm of the Bardi. Both were victims of overextension, and both were caught by the failure of Edward III of England to make good his debts. An international financial crisis ensued, and the Acciaiuoli, the third largest Florentine banking firm, also collapsed. For a time there was financial chaos, but a few firms survived to carry on the traditions of Italian banking and soon new firms arose to fill the places of the old. The trade contraction following the plagues limited both the size and the number of new firms, and even such relative giants of the new era as the Medici did not attain the scale of their predecessors. From the later fourteenth century on, however, Italian banking recovered its primacy even though within a greatly reduced international economy, and the names of the Medici, the Pazzi, the Rucellai, and the Strozzi resounded through the world in the silver age of Italian banking.

As an international institution, drawing its revenues from the most distant outposts of Christianity, the Church required the services of diversified banking firms with far-flung branches in order to transmit funds to the central coffers in Rome. As bullion became scarce and political circumstance rendered the physical transport of specie more hazardous, the services of such banking firms as the Medici became ever more essential for the transfer of papal remittances. In turn, as bankers became more essential, they became more powerful within the hierarchy of the Church and more capable of manipulating ecclesiastical power for their own ends. The Medici, rising from the shambles left by the troubled decades after 1340, quickly perceived the advantages of an association with Rome. Such services as they could offer were richly rewarded in this world; the Medici, until 1434, drew more than half their revenues from their Rome branch, even though their main office was located in Florence. Part of the profits from Church business were derived from the Curia itself—but only a part. Acting as key bankers to the Pope, the Medici naturally acquired the accounts of lesser churchmen—cardinals, bishops, and other affluent ecclesiastics. Such business was particularly successful because the futures, both spiritual and secular, of the lesser clergymen were dependent upon the sanction of the Pope. Since the Pope was himself increasingly dependent upon his bankers, the inevitable occurred and the authority of the papacy was marshaled to guarantee the repayment of loans that the Medici made to subordinate clerics. More dangerous still to the integrity of the Church, the vesting of such power in the hands of the bankers invited corruption and bribery as venal men sought elevation in ecclesiastical office. In at least one case, the Medici withheld the papal bulls which would have elevated an English cleric to the Bishopric of London until his uncle, a cardinal, had settled his debts—his own and those of his nephew. Gradually, excommunication became a fairly common threat against defaulting clerics. Thus the Medici could make loans which, were secured not only by the ordinary moral and legal guarantees, but also by the spiritual and organizational power of the Church itself.

Under such favorable influences, the Medici grew rapidly. From modest origins in the late fourteenth century, the firm quickly developed into a major international force with correspondent banks in all corners of the world. Supplementing the network of correspondents, true branches under the direct control of the main bank were established in major cities from Florence, the headquarters, to Rome, Venice, Naples, Milan, Pisa, Geneva, Lyons, Basel, Avignon, Bruges, and London. During the early fifteenth century, profits and capital soared, but since the Medici favored pomp and display over miserly hoarding, capital accumulation lagged far behind profits. At its peak, according to Raymond de Roover, the modern historian of the bank, Medici capital totaled about 72,000 florins— less than that of either the earlier Bardi or the Peruzzi companies.[3] Banking profits for the 16-year period 1435–50 amounted to over 260,000 florins; another 29,000 florins profit came from the firm's industrial activities during the same period.

At this time, Rome continued to be the most profitable branch,

[3] Raymond de Roover, *Medici Bank,* op. cit.

but the second most successful establishment was at Venice; it yielded 20 per cent of the total in 1450. Our previous discussion of the northern economies suggests some of the reasons for the success of Venice as the closest runner-up to Rome; the taste for luxury goods, so prevalent after the Black Death, was precisely tailored to the economic interests of Venice, the Italian city with the greatest commercial involvement in the Levant trade. It was no accident that the Medici involvement in international trade was greater at this branch than at any other. During its great period in the early fifteenth century, the Medici bank was too sensitive to profitable opportunities to overlook the rewards to be garnered from the trade of Venice when that city held a near monopoly over the Levant trade and when the trade itself was the most active commercial endeavor remaining after the disruptions of the late fourteenth century.

Venice in fact benefited from the crises that ruined others. A long and expensive war with Genoa—the war of the Chioggia, 1378–81—had prostrated the two great trading cities, but Venice possessed greater recuperative powers. The Genoese lost their colonies first in the Levant and then subsequently on the Black Sea, but the Venetians maintained contact with the east, despite the growing Turkish threat, through a combination of military effort and more peaceful negotiation to obtain commercial treaties. This continued contact with the east gave Venice the economic base for rebuilding her luxury trade while world demand was strong. To a considerable degree, this factor alone accounts for the marked difference between her economic history in the later Middle Ages and that of the other maritime states of Italy.

Such success was not accomplished without cost, however, both economic and social. The relentless expansion of the Turks—the south side of the Dardanelles by 1326, both sides by 1354, much of the Balkan Peninsula by 1393, and finally Constantinople itself in 1453—diverted more and more funds from productive activity to defense. At the same time, Venetian territorial expansion into the Adriatic hinterland, prompted by fear of the rising power of Milan and perhaps also by the increasing scarcity of timber, put additional pressure upon state funds and reduced the efficiency of the Italian military effort against the Turk. The Venetian Arsenal, the source of naval power, underwent a fourfold expansion between 1313 and 1325; by 1473, it had doubled again. Escalating taxation paralleled the war expenditures; during the Chioggia period, citizens were forced to loan the state more than 100 per cent of their assessed assets; in the fourth decade of the fifteenth century, the rate grew to nearly 300 per cent. Granted that the assessed values were far below the actual assets of the Venetians, the tax bite was substantial, and it became more onerous as trade began to contract in the latter half of the fifteenth century.

That the Venetians could pay such levies was a tribute to the role of the luxury trade in maintaining the economic vitality of their city. But the payments were not made without considerable social cost, and the degree of social inequality grew as taxes and restrictions combined to prevent the humble from rising. Despite inequalities in the distribution of income—or perhaps because of them— Venice became the unchallenged greatest seaport in the world at the end of the Middle Ages. Huge sums of money—Doge Tomaso Mocenigo in the fourteen-twenties spoke of 1,612,000 ducats— flowed from Lombardy to Venice in search of goods; some commodities, mostly cloth, were added to this, but a great part of the trade involved the actual transfer of cash to Venice. The Lombard trade was but a quarter of the total trade of Venice at the time; yet to this region alone, again following Mocenigo, the city sold more than 1,571,000 ducats worth of products from the eastern Mediterranean. The Doge was justifiably proud of this trade, and in urging its continuation by the avoidance of war, he declared that if the trade prospered, the citizens of Venice would soon become "masters of all the gold in Christendom." The latter phrase was perhaps carefully chosen; according to Mocenigo's estimate, the Venetian mint coined annually 1,000,000 ducats of gold, 200,000 ducats of silver, and 800,000 ducats of minor coin. Such a coinage was an immense sum for a relatively small city-state and exceeded the combined coinages of England and France in most of the first 60 years of the fifteenth century. Yet there was apparently no very pronounced inflation—the normal consequence of excessively large mint outputs—that could have absorbed such vast issues. Where did the money go? A good deal, as we have already observed, went to military and diplomatic expenses and some undoubtedly went into private hoards. If the Doge was even approximately correct in his figures, however, a great portion of the annual coinage was promptly exported. Mocenigo, in explaining the distribution of the coinage, allots 500,000 ducats annually to Syria alone. The contemporary Arab commentator Ibn Taghri Birdi independently confirms the Doge's words, and notes that the *ifranti* (Arabic for "ducat" or "florin") became the common coin of all the major cities "such as Cairo, Old Cairo, Syria, Asia Minor, the East, Hijaz, and Yemen." [4] In 1425, the Egyptian dinar was debased to match the weight of the great quantities of Italian coins then circulating in Egypt. The most recent research suggests that the vast tide of Italian coin flowed from Egypt to India and beyond, to the farther east.

But let us consider the economic implications of the trade of Venice in the broader European context. Purveyor of luxuries to the world, Venice was able to draw immense sums to herself, without actually producing much in the way of real goods. According to the Doge, some 42,000 men were employed either as seamen or shipbuilders, compared to 3,000 in the silk industry and 16,000 in the fustian industry. Thus a very large portion of the population was more involved in the transport of goods than in their production. Venice herself did not produce enough to balance her trade with the east, and although she did re-export some goods of Lombard and northern European manufacture, not enough such goods were sold to balance the accounts with the Levant. As a result, Venice siphoned vast sums away from the countries to her north and west and channeled them to the east. In this way, she contributed directly to the monetary phase of the post-plague recession which distressed the other economies of Europe, and she built for herself a magnificent but temporary affluence at the expense of others.

Although Venice was dominant among Italian trading cities, Genoa did not collapse. Progressively cut off from her former colonies to the east, she directed her attention to substitute markets in the west, to heavier goods, to new markets in central Europe, and to the military demands among the hostile nations confronting each

[4] Quoted in William Popper, *Egypt and Syria under the Circassian Sultans, 1382–1468* (Berkeley and Los Angeles: University of California Press, 1957), p. 47.

other in the north. Genoese ships were maintained and offered for hire to northern monarchs and others who required navies. War profiteers thus found gain even in a period of trade contraction; archers and soldiers risked their lives to earn the gold of the north. On the other hand, however, such substitutes for legitimate economic activity were at best only makeshift endeavors to recoup losses suffered elsewhere. Merchants with viable commercial interests do not ordinarily divert their ships to warlike ends, nor do men who sense the opportunity to climb to commercial heights seek employment as foot soldiers. Bulky goods, as we have observed, were no replacement for the spices and luxuries of the east—particularly at a time when the luxury trade was the only lively and expanding international market. Despite the efforts to restore trade to its vigorous late thirteenth-century levels, the commerce of Genoa faded throughout the later Middle Ages, and if an occasional Genoese did find prosperity, it was often the result of noncommercial activity. Some success certainly was found in silk manufacturing, in the provision of fancy fruits to rich northerners, and to some extent in the trade with the Iberian Peninsula, but as Graph VI (p. 130) shows, such activity was not sufficient to halt the steady erosion of prosperity. By 1405, the Genoese state was virtually bankrupt, and in fact, the state's debt-holders in that year formed a private corporation to protect their interests and to manage the public revenues.

Venice, through the Levant trade, and Milan, through armaments, became exceptions to the general malaise that afflicted trade and industry throughout much of Europe, but their success was only temporary, depending as it did upon economic conditions which could not last. Northern bullion resources could not endure forever without being replenished, and Venetian galleys and Genoese carracks could not long continue to carry much gold and little cargo away from the north without ultimately destroying the trade. Even during the peak periods of luxury sales, several Italian cities sensed danger and acted, although without great success, to curb the tendency toward high living and low productivity. The Venetian sumptuary law of 1360 specifically complains that money spent on inordinate luxury was detracting from productive investment in shipping and industry. In other Italian cities throughout the fourteenth and fifteenth centuries, similar pronouncements were incorporated into the sumptuary laws, but the statements that expenditures of the rich were impoverishing the cities seem to have had a double meaning; such expenditures not only reduced investment, but they also caused the export of funds. Even in Italy, few cities were, like Venice, located astride a river of gold. In Italy, as elsewhere, restrictionism grew during the later Middle Ages, but it was powerless to prevent the ultimate effects of an unstable economic base from being felt.

In the north, the gradual exhaustion of money supplies and the increasing efforts of princes to substitute domestic for imported manufactures and to limit the importation of southern luxuries worked against continued Italian prosperity in those fortunate cities favored by the luxury trade. With the conclusion of the Hundred Years' War in 1453, both the northern economies and the northern princes became more powerful and could compete more effectively against the Italian hegemony in international trade. In the eastern Mediterranean at the same time, Turkish forces were triumphant; the collapse of Constantinople in 1453 rendered access to the eastern markets simultaneously more difficult and more expensive. Both Egyptians and Turks increased their tariffs and their prices, wielding their duopoly of the eastern trade for all it was worth. The Venetians were caught in the middle. During the initial period of post-plague affluence, when fear of death appeared to justify any expense in the name of pleasure, costs could readily be passed along to the consumer, but by the middle of the fifteenth century, the luxury market seems to have weakened as both population and domestic food prices rose, limiting the free funds available for luxury consumption, and as northern stocks of precious metals waned. Costs of trade were rising, and they had now to be absorbed by the trader. In addition, the Turkish naval threat was stronger than ever—one chronicler describes the masts of the Turkish fleet as a forest moving across the water—and exhaustion of the timber supply was raising both the cost and the difficulty of maintaining a competitive naval force. Under these combined influences, the Italian cities and commercial enterprises which had weathered the crises of the later fourteenth century and, in a few instances, even profited from them, fell upon hard times. The late fifteenth century was a

bleak period for Venice. In 1463, the outbreak of violent war between Venice and the Turks resulted in the massacre of all the Venetians then resident in Turkey; 13 years of outright war followed.
Venice thus found that her supply of eastern goods was cut off and,
at the same time, that her northern markets were badly eroded. She
began to return to productive industry, notably cloth manufacture,
in the sixteenth century, but the transition from her role as entrepôt
was painful. In Florence as well, that bellweather of Florentine
economic activity the Medici bank was clearly slipping by 1460. A
major banking crisis, the worst since the catastrophe that destroyed
the Bardi and the Peruzzi in the thirteen-forties, struck Florence in
1464–65 and from that time, the Medici exercised a defensive policy
of contraction, eliminating less profitable branches whenever possible. Though the bank endured until the fourteen-nineties, the
great period of vitality was over. The late fifteenth century was a
gloomy period for Italy, when even those portions of the country
that had maintained their affluence at the beginning declined at
the close of the century. Some recovery was indeed made—one may
cite Venetian success in the cloth industry and Genoa's financial
renaissance in the service of Spain—but Italy never again regained
the dominant position she had held in the world's economy during
the Middle Ages.

BEYOND GIBRALTAR

To a great extent the geographical revolution and the technological factors that supported it were responsible for this failure. From
the thirteenth century onward, sailing ships had been improving
in design. The square sail of the north, with its limited maneuver-
ability in sailing close to the wind was supplemented by the lateen
sail of the Mediterranean south. The resultant ship could point
better than its northern predecessors, and yet it retained the advantages that the square rig offered in the divisibility of canvas
during storms and in the possibility of extending the sail area without exceeding the natural limits imposed on the lateen rig by the
length and weight of the single yard. More maneuverable and more
seaworthy ships were then becoming available in the fifteenth cen-

tury and, of even greater significance, they could be handled by smaller crews. The ships could thus travel farther from land, both because of improved design and because it had become feasible to carry adequate provisions for an extended voyage. Since the medieval oared galley normally made nightly landings along the shores of the Mediterranean, the ratio between the number of crewmen and the size of the hold was not of prime importance. The new ships could remain self-sufficient at sea for long periods—a crucial factor in the conquest of the Atlantic.

Technology, in the absence of the desire to apply it, has little value. Medieval men, however, had long exhibited considerable geographical curiosity; exploration, albeit by land and in the east, pushed forward during the thirteenth century. In the early years of that century, missions had been sent to convert the Great Khan to Christianity, and despite their failure, the accounts of the travelers, particularly those of the secular hero, Marco Polo, stimulated the imagination of western Europeans. Rumors of Japan and of the riches of the far eastern coast drifted back to Europe, and before 1300, explorers had set forth to reach the Far East by sea. The ill-fated expedition of the Vivaldi brothers in 1291 was never heard from again after it passed the Straits of Gibraltar, but their courageous attempt shows that men were then ready to face the dangers of the wider Atlantic, known on the maps of the time only as the Green Sea of Darkness. The early fourteenth century, the period that saw the opening of the direct sea routes from Italy to Flanders, witnessed further encounters with the wider Atlantic. As early as 1344, the Kingdom of Castile claimed, and had extracted from the papacy, a title to the Canary Islands, off the coast of Africa. It is probable that the Azores and the Madeiras were known by that date as well. Little was done either to push discovery further or to exploit the known islands during the latter half of the fourteenth century. Perhaps the problems associated with the plague and the depopulation and economic contraction that followed in its wake rendered any further exploration infeasible. Here, as in many other scientific and technological areas, the most promising developments of the early years of the fourteenth century suffered a rather abrupt period of arrest after the plague.

By the early fifteenth century, however, a coalition of forces reactivated the interest in the Atlantic. The success of such Italian cities as Venice in drawing Europe's bullion resources to herself drove the gold-starved north to seek new sources of precious metal. From early times, gold had come from Senegal overland across northwest Africa; it was not long before Europeans realized that they could profit greatly if they could bypass this route and find the southern source of the yellow metal. From the political side as well, events urged Europeans to turn their attention from the eastern to the western Mediterranean and to the Atlantic. The increasing difficulty of negotiating with the Egyptians and the steady progress of the Turks left less and less opportunity for profit in the eastern Mediterranean and, by threatening the supply lines to spices, silks, and other eastern commodities, stimulated interest in alternative passages. Dim rumors of a Christian kingdom in the east raised false hopes of an alliance between the forces of western Christendom and the eastern kingdom of Prester John and speculation on the launching of a pincer movement to crush the Turks.

By the early fifteenth century, the stimuli for discovery existed in strength, and the technological capability was at hand. The task was undertaken by Portugal, a small kingdom seemingly bypassed by the greater trends of the Middle Ages but one possessing considerable advantages for her fifteenth-century role. Portugal, of course, faced the Atlantic and, since she was at once the southern terminus of the Hanseatic trade route across the northern coast of Europe and a way station in the galley trade from Italy to Flanders, she was exposed to both southern and northern sources of technology and sea lore. Equally important, since Portugal was located on the outer fringes of Europe, she avoided many of Europe's most pressing political problems; the entire Mediterranean and the combined forces of the southern Christian powers acted as a buffer for her against the Turk. She was too small to be significantly involved in the struggle between France and England and too remote to be affected by the northern conflicts of the Hanse against the Poles and other Baltic powers. Perhaps as important, although some would take issue, Portugal was to some extent isolated from the dominant cultural development of Europe during the fifteenth century. As a result, while the southern portions of Europe were rediscovering antiquity and substituting the authority of the classics for experimental empiricism, the Portuguese were combining practical experience, Arab science, and open inquiry in an eclectic approach to the problems of the Atlantic.

The familiar Chinese proverb says that a journey of a thousand leagues begins with one short step; Portugal took that short step in 1415, when John I and his sons conquered Ceuta, a Moorish fortress on the southern side of the Straits of Gibraltar. Within a century that step opened the path to China. The town was held as a Portuguese fortress and became a base for future African expeditions. To some extent, the victory was no more than a logical stage in the long reconquest of the Iberian Peninsula from the Arabs, and there was certainly a strong element of the medieval Crusade in the motivation for the attack. On the other hand, since the town was thereafter held and garrisoned by Portugal—a single state acting *as* a state—there were then also in this venture visible elements of modern colonialism. Henceforth the economic organization of foreign trade would be on an even grander scale than that practiced by the Italian city-states, requiring the intervention and power of national bodies; individual merchants or even groups of merchants seeking privileges in foreign countries were too small to undertake the risks, costs, and military commitments that would be necessary in the unfolding new world.

At the same time as they took Ceuta, the Portuguese were also involved with Castile in a scramble for the offshore islands. Castile was able to make good her claim to the Canaries, but the Azores and the Madeiras fell to Portugal: they were to provide both a base and, as we shall see, an economic rationale for further exploration. These initial successes encouraged additional efforts, and Portugal, under the leadership of Prince Henry the Navigator, King John's son, began to probe farther along the African coast in search of gold and the commodities that could win gold. Progress was slow, hindered by fear of the unknown and by fantastic rumors, largely based on the imaginative extrapolation of readily observable phenomena—if the sea became ever warmer as one sailed south, did it not become a boiling caldron in the unexplored regions? But progress by sea was reasonably steady and each additional venture forced men to realize that their fears were exaggerated. By 1434, Cape Bojador was rounded, and by 1446, Cape Verde and the mouth of the Senegal River had been reached. Perhaps more important in determining the future than the allaying of ignorant fear, the profitability of African exploitation had been established by mid-century, and a permanent Portuguese trading station had been founded at Arguin on the West African coast. The slave trade began in earnest during the fourth decade of the fifteenth century, and the direct transport of West African slaves replaced the older trans-Saharan traffic. By 1433, Henry the Navigator had specifically authorized the capture of slaves in the regions surrounding Cape Bojador; within the next decade, the Portuguese crown had demanded a fifth of the revenues earned in the slave trade, and the commerce was thus embedded in the Portuguese fiscal system. With the increasing colonization of the Atlantic islands and the developing awareness of their profitability when turned to sugar and wine cultivation, the market for West African slaves expanded. Almost from the beginning, the discovery of the Atlantic was associated with the slave trade. The fuller opening of the New World made the demand greater still, and while certainly exaggerated, there is yet an oblique element of truth in the charge leveled by one French historian that the great Christopher Columbus was the true founder of the slave trade. The history of the economic exploitation of the Atlantic archipelagoes and the Americas lies beyond the purview of this volume, but even the earliest development of these discoveries had economic significance for Europe. It will be recalled that one of the chief responses of Sicilian wheat growers to the shrinkage of demand following depopulation and plague was the development of a specialized agriculture, centered on such luxury crops as sweet wines and sugar. By the middle of the fifteenth century, the Atlantic islands were raising precisely these crops in competition with the Mediterranean sources of supply; grown on highly fertile soil with relatively cheap slave labor, the competitive products of the Atlantic made a dramatic and irreversible impact upon the European market. Before the century was over, the Portuguese had found it necessary to establish export quotas on sugar in order to maintain the European price. Mediterranean agriculture could not compete under such circumstances, and henceforth the agrarian south of Italy became an underdeveloped and poor region, unable to regain the lost glory of the high Middle Ages, when it had been the breadbasket of the flourishing Italian city-states.

Once the profitability of the explorations had been proved, however, nothing could restrain further progress; the southward and westward voyages grew more and more daring. A second Portuguese trading station was founded at Elmina on the Gold Coast in 1482; it soon became the center of a brisk trade in slaves, ivory, gold, and even a coarse variety of pepper. West African pepper was an inferior variety, but even if it was not comparable in quality, it provided an alternative to the more expensive eastern spice. Consequently, the price of West African pepper, plus a differential premium reflecting relative quality, set an upper limit to the price of the best eastern grades. One of the most valuable items of the traditional Italian trading monopoly thus became subject to competition even before the Cape of Good Hope was rounded. The strategic monopoly of the Italians was weakened in the fifteenth century; by the beginning of the sixteenth century, the last vestiges of Italian geographical advantage had been destroyed by the triumph of Bartholomew Dias and his successors, who opened the sea route to India and the Spice Islands beyond.

5

Government, Property, and the Individual

1

For the articulate and talented few, the Renaissance was a period of opportunity, a time of intellectual upward mobility. It was also to become, however, an era that challenged the traditional hierarchical structure of society and substituted new concepts of social merit for the older, medieval values, which, though not completely rigid, yielded only slowly to change. True, a man of talent and grace could find fortune and reputation—in short, magnificence— more readily in the Renaissance, but, once the stable hierarchy that had guaranteed his humble security was shaken, what was to become of the ordinary being with clumsy hands and dull wits? In retrospect, let us consider that we began with the human soul and the protection of the rights of the individual man in the thirteenth century, and we have arrived at the expansion of the slave trade and a growing trend toward political absolutism in the fifteenth. What were the elements of change and how did they interact?

It is a truism that social change is immensely complex and that it proceeds on many interwoven levels—intellectual, political, religious, artistic, and economic; no simple explanation, no single catalyst, is ever entirely convincing. But in the case of the Renaissance, many scholars have exhibited a curious aversion against recognizing first the fact, and then the inseparability, of the interconnections among the various forms of social consciousness and activity. But all factors were relevant, and their interactions both real and intense. Too often, for example, the march of Church history, from the hypothetical apex of Catholic unity in the thirteenth century to the nadir of Reformation confusion in the sixteenth, is viewed primarily as a problem of internal doctrinal strife, fanned perhaps by fresh intellectual winds from the newly recovered classics. Both the submerged and the evident economic factors at work are dismissed with a reference to the sale of indulgences, or, in the best work, with some reference to the Church's need for funds; but that is not enough. Too often, also, the history of secular political thought is studied as a phenomenon only of abstractions, and not as a continuous and dynamic attempt by living men to understand and get control over the urgent, frequently dirty and ignoble problems of their times. Yet it is more than a little doubtful that the course of political thought from Dante to Machiavelli would have been unaffected by the base economic pressures and the shifts of economic power that occurred in the interim that separates them. Economic forces had their impact upon every aspect, real as well as theoretical, of the world of the later Middle Ages and early Renaissance, but they in turn did not exist in a vacuum; obviously, it is as silly to distort historical change by a simple-minded economic determinism as it is to overlook or minimize the importance of economics. Many factors combined to alter the position of the individual and the conception and actual power of governments over the course of the fourteenth and fifteenth centuries. It has been our task to describe some of the changes in emphasis and interest that affected both man and the state as *economic* entities in the larger structure of an evolving society. Let us now briefly expand the context.

Renaissance Humanism—the recovery of Latin learning—indeed dramatized, as the textbook cliché runs, "man" as the center of the universe, but "man" means here the highly cultivated, sensitive, and graceful paragon of the Renaissance, and not "man" the all-encompassing medieval common noun that generously includes all ranks, no matter how humble, so long as they be Christian. If the study of Latin letters modified the concept of the ideal and the individual, it also produced a revived interest in Roman law. The Corpus Juris Civilis, the sixth-century compilation of Roman law, was simultaneously the legislative remains of an absolute government with an obvious bias in favor of the absolute prince, and a body of received law that could be used to oppose customary law.

It was thus hostile to the traditional medieval liberties and privileges generated and defended by extended practice. Humanistic study, then, began to produce a philosophic and legal bias towards absolutism, and encouraged the more vigorous application of Roman law, a powerful device to implement that propensity, by undermining traditional constraints that limited monarchies and protected the meek. By the sixteenth century, historical scholarship, another precocious child of Humanism, demonstrated that even the Corpus Juris itself was subject to question, since it was revealed to be merely a compilation of Roman laws of various periods, and not a timeless statement of the optimal law of an ideal society at its peak. Thus, even such limited constraining power as the Corpus Juris might impose upon the prince was eroded, and abstract law —even the idea of abstract law—diminished in importance as an impediment to the free exercise of princely ego.

In a parallel development, the internal problems of the Church effectively reduced the role of that body as a constraining force on princes. The Babylonian Captivity and then the Schism first reduced the spiritual prestige of the Church and then attacked its organizational integrity. The Schism, by dividing the Church's revenues among its fragments, lowered the concerted power of the whole. Conciliarism—the effort to settle the Schism by appealing to the authority of the presumably indivisible whole body of the church—popularized semidemocratic ideas that were in effect inconsistent with the continuing authority of the Pope. By challenging the role of the Pope within the Church, such ideas, although ultimately rejected, diminished the possibilities of papal intervention outside the Church to counterbalance the growth of monarchical power. Simultaneously, historical scholarship, textual criticism, and the growth of secular literacy raised doubts about the interpretation of the basic sources of ecclesiastical power—the Bible and the canon law. Heresy, which had always plagued the Church, became more virulent; by the fifteenth and early sixteenth centuries, when doubt was more general, it could be used to forward the worldly aims of secular princes engaged in the construction of national states. The monarch could use the divisive influence of heresy as well as the actual political support of anticlerical forces to undermine the power of the Church. Restraints shrank as the glory of the state grew.

In political theory, the tendencies of Humanism and heresy combined. From the time of Marsilius of Padua, whose *Defensor Pacis* in 1324 led to his prompt excommunication, increasingly articulate statements were made which asserted the unity of secular power within the state—there could be but one authority—and located that power in the prince. Some variants sought to find parallels in political theory to the conciliar theory of the Church and thus to limit the monarchy through an appeal to the whole body of the people; but such attempts were relatively frail, and while a continuous undertone throughout the fifteenth and sixteenth centuries, they were never the dominant theme of the political theory of that era.

Beginning to coalesce from many sides, then, the intellectual currents of the later Middle Ages and the early Renaissance urged greater power upon secular monarchies and challenged the traditional limits that custom, the Church, canon and divine law, and even the reciprocal nature of the contract implicit in feudalism had placed upon the prince. Yet such challenges were not entirely new. To understand the unique success of secular princes in capitalizing on them during the fifteenth century, we must certainly include the changes in the economic environment which increasingly strengthened the independence of the few and the subjugation of the many.

2

Throughout western Europe, restrictionism grew, and government was increasingly called upon to intrude in economic affairs. Depopulation and the rapid relocation of the survivors led monarchs and other secular rulers to intervene in urban affairs and to overrule petty town legislation in favor of more national interests. Pressing difficulties among craftsmen made them an easy and willing prey for greater monarchical control, so long as it promised to alleviate their troubles; unfortunately for them, it was easier to impose controls than to restore prosperity. Within the guilds themselves, the same rule applied; the restrictionism of the fourteenth, and particularly of the fifteenth, century instituted a more rigorous pattern of vertical control, and this in turn, once the guilds appealed to national authority, cleared the way for governmental domination.

Labor shortages resulting from the plague produced petitions for wage legislation both in agriculture and in manufacturing throughout Europe. Each new demand, supported as it was by a substantial segment of the economic community, further opened the way for princes to establish precedents and mechanisms for the direct control of the individual worker. The complex of wage controls, mandatory labor requirements, and limitations on geographical mobility collectively redefined the relationship between the ordinary individual and the government. These tendencies were reinforced by the almost universal problem of specie flows and the international balance of payments. Individual freedom was circumscribed by legislation that forbade the export of money, required foreign merchants to purchase specified quantities of native goods, authorized the inspection of departing travelers, demanded that owners of bullion and plate carry it to the royal mints, and which in one case even urged hostelers to search their guests in an effort to prevent the smuggling of coin. Imbalances in the international accounts led as well to the widespread publication of sumptuary laws which, whether they failed or succeeded in their intent, brought national government even more directly into the regulation of the lives of individual citizens.

The enlarged scale of warfare in the later Middle Ages contributed to the monetary scarcity and forced governments to seek new sources of funds to meet the growing expense of new technology, mercenary forces, and more extensive campaigns. Fiscal necessity thus compelled governments everywhere to invade individual pockets and establish precedents for additional direct taxation either peacefully or, more often, by the suppression of rebellion and the consequent destruction of legal as well as illegal resistance. The tempting accumulations of ecclesiastical wealth drew the attention of monarchs and princes alike, while the role of the Church as an exporter of scarce money mobilized the anticlerical support of the bullion-starved townspeople in favor of the government. Taxation of the Church became less politically dangerous when large segments of the population supported it; at the same time, the controls imposed by royal authority on papal remittances involved the Crown directly in internal ecclesiastical affairs.

The Church, of course, resisted, but economic circumstance favored the government. As a landlord, the Church suffered from declining rents and falling agricultural prices which weakened its economic power base. At the same time, since labor legislation had to be national to attain even its limited effectiveness, the economic interests of the Church coincided with those of ordinary landlords in allowing, indeed inviting, increased royal regulation of the labor force resident on ecclesiastical fiefs. That such laws failed in their purpose was probably a benefit to the rising monarchies, since the fact of royal control was established without substantially altering the continuous drain upon the economic resources of both clerical and lay landlords.

Exploration of the Atlantic, by vastly enlarging the known world, favored a corresponding growth in monarchical power. Mariners from the Italian city-states might lend their considerable skills to these ventures, but henceforth, national monarchies alone could muster the resources of population and money required for the maintenance of Atlantic colonies. In turn, the colonies rewarded the monarchs with sources of wealth unencumbered by traditional medieval limitations, be they clerical or feudal—sources whose legal status was unclear and whose heathen citizens were outside the protection of the Church. Efforts to assure humane treatment and conversion of the savages were supported by the Church, but the economic interests of the conquerors long remained dominant over the muted demands of the Rome-centered church, whose voice was often rendered conveniently inaudible by distance.

The opening of the western hemisphere dramatized the changed conception of the world. Medieval maps emphasized the theocratic conception of the medieval universe by placing Jerusalem in the geometric center of a circular design, but as Portuguese and Spanish sailors pressed ever westward and southward, these maps became obsolete. It was increasingly difficult to incorporate the new information without destroying the philosophical conception of the old geography. The circle first became an ellipse, and then, overwhelmed by the rapid accumulation of new lands, finally exploded, forever destroying the medieval geographical unity and perfection —substituting a world of empirical fact for the traditional world of spiritual integrity.

Economic and demographic crises both allowed and demanded the increased involvement of governments in every aspect of economic life and simultaneously weakened those segments of medieval society which had limited the arbitrary action of princes. The discoveries altered the very conception of the world and, in time, shattered many of the philosophical assumptions of the Middle Ages. As government grew in stature, the ordinary individual diminished; as the limits to power grew more vague, the place of that individual was challenged; as taxation and economic regulation became more impersonal and less limited, the distinction between public and private grew cloudy, and the justification of private property was less clear. Economic and intellectual trends coalesced, reinforcing each other in their common leaning toward absolutism, but it was the critical failure of the medieval economy to preserve its health during the fourteenth century that allowed secular authorities to dominate European economic systems, to bleed them with an efficiency unknown in the Middle Ages, and to suppress the rights of man beneath the banner of *raison d'état.*

Suggestions for Further Reading

General, with extensive topical bibliographies:

POSTAN, M. M., ed., *The Agrarian Life of the Middle Ages. Cambridge Economic History of Europe*, I (2nd ed.). Cambridge: Cambridge University Press, 1966.

POSTAN, M. M., and E. E. RICH, eds., *Trade and Industry in the Middle Ages. Cambridge Economic History of Europe*, II. Cambridge: Cambridge University Press, 1952.

POSTAN, M. M., E. E. RICH, and EDWARD MILLER, eds., *Economic Organization and Policies in the Middle Ages. Cambridge Economic History of Europe*, III. Cambridge: Cambridge University Press, 1963.

Specific or regional:

DUBY, GEORGES, *Rural Economy and Country Life in the Medieval West*. Columbia, S.C.: University of South Carolina Press, 1968.

FAVIER, JEAN, *Les Finances pontificales a l'époque du grand schisme d'Occident, 1378–1409*. Paris: Éditions E. de Boccard, 1966.

LOPEZ, R. S., and I. W. RAYMOND, *Medieval Trade in the Mediterranean World, Illustrative Documents Translated with Introductions and Notes*. New York and London: Columbia University Press, 1961.

LUZZATTO, GINO, *An Economic History of Italy from the Fall of the Roman Empire to the Beginning of the Sixteenth Century*. New York: Barnes & Noble, Inc., 1961.

PIRENNE, HENRI, *Early Democracies in the Low Countries*. New York, Evanston, and London: Harper and Row, Publishers, 1963.

DE ROOVER, RAYMOND, *The Rise and Decline of the Medici Bank, 1397–1494*. Cambridge, Mass.: Harvard University Press, 1963.

VAN BATH, B. H. SLICHER, *The Agrarian History of Western Europe, A.D. 500–1850*. London: Edward Arnold, Ltd., 1963.

171

Index

Absolutism, 6, 166, 170
Acciaiuoli, 151
Acorns, fodder, 158
Adriatic, 16
Africa, 67, 117, 159–60
Agincourt, Battle of (1415), 9
Albi, pop., 76, 87
Alcira, pop., 76
Alexandria, jewel trade, 128
Alfonso of Castile, 62
Alps, 15, 16
Alum, 97, 126
Amber, 125, 138, 143
Americas, 162
Amsterdam, cloth, 101
Anagni, capture of Pope, 12
Anjou, Duke of, 78
Apulia, 23
Aquinas, Thomas, property and political theory, 2–3
Arab: conquest, 65; trade, 116; science, 161
Aragon, guilds, 110
Arguin, Portuguese colony, 162
Armagnacs, 11
Armies, size, 51
Armor, 124
Arsenal, Venetian, 82, 153
Asia, silk, 104
Asia Minor: 14, 155; silk, 104; alum, 126
Atlantic: 15, 25, 160; cloth markets, 102; coast, 133; conquest of, 159; exploration, 169; islands, 162
Augsburg: 111; clothiers, 101; guilds, 110

Avignon: 5, 145–46; Medici branch, 152
Azores, 159, 161

Babylonian Captivity (1305–78), 5, 145, 166
Balance of payments, 12, 54, 90, 91, 114, 136, 138–58, 168
Balance of trade, and wool, 125
Balkan Peninsula: 14, 23; Turkish control of, 153
Baltic, 101, 117, 123, 138, 143, 160
Bank, Medici, 104; see also Medici
Bankers, 93, 151
Barcelona, pop., 76
Bardi: 121; failure, 151–52, 158
Barley, 35–39, 55
Basel, Medici branch, 152
Bavaria, 148
Beer, 32, 35–36, 38, 40, 58
Beeswax, 125
Bergen, 58–60
Berlin, 75
Birdi, Ibn Taghri, 155
Black Death, 27–28, 34, 41–42, 44, 55, 73, 77, 89, 93, 102, 134, 138, 148, 153
Black Sea: 17, 23, 27, 125, 153; fur, 101; silk, 104
Boccaccio, 87
Bohemia, mining, 114
Bojador, Cape, 161–62
Bologna, silk, 103, 127
Boniface VII, Pope, 1, 4–5
Bordeaux: wine, 51, 133–34; guilds, 108
Bosnia, gold mines, 114
Bourges, guilds, 108

Bourgneuf, Bay of, salt, 123
Brabant, 100–102
Bracelets, 128
Bread, 39, 86
Bremen, pop., 81
Brie, 53
Brocades, 102, 128, 136–37
Bruges, 26, 92, 97, 125, 133, 138, 142, 152
Bullion, 138–39, 141, 144, 146, 148–51, 156, 160, 168
Burgundians, *vs.* Armagnacs, 11
Burgundy, 101, 148, 150
Buriana, pop., 76
Butter, 32, 38, 40, 59–60, 67, 86, 143

Cadsand, Battle of (1337), 93
Caffa, 27
Cairo, 155
Calais, 58
Cambridge, Statute of (1388), 45
Cañadas, 62
Canals, 71
Canary Islands, 159, 161
Candles, 125
Carpathian Mountains, 14
Carpenter, 83
Carting, 45
Caspian Sea, 117
Castellon, pop., 76
Castile, 93, 110, 148, 159, 161
Castle Combe, 47, 84
Catalonia, pop., 28–29, 31
Caucasus, 15
Cereals, 45
Ceuta, 161
Champagne, Counts of, 116–17
Champagne fairs, 117, 119, 132–33
Charlemagne, 92, 116
Charles V (1364–80), 53, 56, 78, 85, 107, 131
Charles VI (1380–1422), 107
Charles VII (1422–61), 11, 107–8, 122
Chaucer, Geoffrey, 135
Cheese, 38
China, 104, 126, 161
Chioggia, War of (1378–81), 153–54
Chiompi uprising, 102, 106
Cipolla, Carlo, 69
Citrus, 91
Clement V, Pope, 5

Clericis laicos, 5
Climate, 15–16, 18–19, 33, 72
Cloth: 34, 47, 82, 92, 94, 136, 142; coarse, 71; Flemish, 64, 124; gold and silver, 103, 127; industry, 95, 100, 102, 110; Lombard, 154; making, 63, 124, 127, 158; silk, 105; trade, 94
Clothiers, 97
Cloth workers, 98–99
Coeur, Jacques, 122, 150
Coin: export prohibited, 150; smuggling, 168
Coinage: 141; debasement, 10, 40, 53; gold, 139; silver, 139–40; Venetian, 154
Cologne, 143
Colonies, 169
Colonization, 19, 21
Columbus, Christopher, 162
Commenda, 118, 122
Commutation of labor service, 60
Conciliarism, 166
Constance, Council of (1415), 114
Constantinople: 119; pop., 73; trade, 125; Turkish, 153, 157
Corpus Juris Civilis, 165–66
Courtrai, Battle of (1302), 1, 9
Craftsmen, 111–12
Crecy, Battle of (1346), 9
Credit, 57, 59, 69, 112, 119–22
Crop rotation: 17–18; and legumes, 38
Crusades, 116, 161
Curia, papal, 152
Custom, 167
Customs, 133; *see also* Duties, Tariffs
Cuxham, wheat prices, 26
Cyprus, 128

Dairy: farming, 58; goods, 38
Dalmatian coast, 79, 125
Dante, 10, 165
Danube Basin, 14
Danzig, 143
Damasks, 102, 127
Dardanelles, 153
Dauphiné, 55
Debasement, coinage, 10, 40, 53
Decameron, 87

Defensor Pacis, 6, 167
Demesne, 42–43
Denmark, 15, 100
Devon, silver mines, 113
Dias, Bartholomew, 163
Dieppe, trade, 129–30
Diplomacy, expense, 148, 154
Discoveries, 169–70
Domesday Survey (1086), 19
Duby, Georges, 44
Du Guesclin, Bertrand, 51
Durham, Bishop of, 47
Dutch: Baltic, 101; fishermen, 123
Duties: 6; cloth, 99; death, 145
Dyestuffs, 32, 57, 68, 71, 126–27

East Anglia, 96
Écus, 54
Edward I (1272–1307), 1, 4, 5, 92
Edward II (1307–27), 78
Edward III (1327–77), 12, 64, 92, 95, 121, 143, 145, 151
Eggs, 38
Egypt, 117, 155
Egyptians, 157, 160
Elbe, 61, 136
Elmina, Portuguese colony, 163
Emigration, in famine, 27
England: 18, 25, 29, 31, 50–51, 53–58, 61, 64, 78, 90, 93, 98, 99, 105, 121–22, 124, 137–38, 143, 160; agriculture, 32–51; cloth, 94, 95, 97, 100, 137; coinage, 139, 154; diplomatic expense, 148; famine, 26; forests, 16; import restrictions, 142; pop., 28, 75; price indices, 89; rents, 44; silver mines, 113; sumptuary laws, 136; topography, 15; trade, 129–30; wheat prices, 26; wine, 123, 134; wool, 92, 96, 126
Engrossing, 77
Epidemics, 27, 29
Epizootics, 40
Exchange contract, 118–19, 122, 142
Exchange rates: 120; fixed, 141
Excommunication, 2, 5, 152
Exports: balance imports, 137, 148–49; embargoes, 6, 93, 97, 100, 102, 149–50; of money, 157, 168; wine, 134

Fairs: Champagne, 117, 119, 132; Geneva, 133; Lyons, 133
Famine: 23, 26, 55, 66, 70, 81, 87, 112; (1315–17), 1, 25, 78, 80; and health, 27; and skill, 83
Fastolf, Sir John, 47, 84
Favier, Jean, 146
Fertilization, 24
Feudalism: contract, 167; economic, 57
Finance, 74
Fir, 123
Fishing, 58–59, 123, 137
Flanders: 1, 51, 63, 80, 93–94, 96, 98, 100, 123, 148, 159, 160; Count of, 4; cloth, 64, 97; coinage, 141; monetary restrictions, 150; towns, 74; trade, 116; wool, 12, 105
Flax, 57, 71
Florence: 85, 92, 99, 158; Ciompi Revolt, 106; cloth, 94, 98, 102; food for, 23; Medici, 152; pop., 73, 75–76; silk, 103–4, 127
Forestalling, 77
Forests, 16, 58, 124
Forncett, revenues, 47
France: 18, 51–53, 55–57, 69, 78, 89, 92, 106, 119, 121–22, 137, 160; coinage, 139; diplomatic expense, 148; famine, 26; forests, 16; guilds, 110; Italians bypass, 133; ivory, 126; market for grain, 66; new villagers, 19; plague, 28; rents, 30; salt, 123; silk, 103; specie exports, 146; sumptuary laws, 136; topography, 14–15; trade, 117
Franconia, 57
Frankfurt, 144
Franzesi, Ciampolo, and Musciatto, 121
Frederick II, 3–4
Freedom, 61, 168
Fuggers, 122
Fullers: 82–83, 96–99; earth, 97
Furs, 60, 101, 124, 136–38, 142–43
Fustian, 155

Gascony: confiscated, 4; salt, 133; wine, 123, 133
Geneva fairs, 133
Genoa: 118, 144, 155; food for, 23;

Genoa *(cont.)*
> Medici branch, 152; and Spain, 158; trade, 125, 129–30; war with Venice, 153

Germany: 15, 18, 53, 57, 59–60, 70, 72, 143; arms, 128; bankers, 122; cloth, 100, 101, 127; forests, 16; 84; guilds, 110; mining, 150; money export, 147; silk, 103; silver, 114; southern, 102, 111; towns, 74; trade, 101, 125

Gerona, pop., 76

Ghent: 92, 97; famine, 26; pop., 74

Gibraltar, Straits of, 133, 159, 161

Ginger, 127

Gisors, guilds, 108

Gold: 54, 144, 156, 161; African, 163; coin, 120, 122, 139, 154; export, 134, 138, 146, 150; production, 114; Senegal, 160

Gold Coast, 163

Good Hope, Cape of, 163

Gracechurch, 78

Granada, 65

Greece, 14

Gregory IX, Pope, 3

Grève, 78

Guilds: 98, 106, 109, 111, 167; cloth, 97; France, 107; officers, 110; regulation, 12

Haarlem, cloth, 101

Halles, 78

Hamburg, pop., 81

Hanse: 58–59, 100, 101, 138, 143–44, 160; coin export, 143; fishing, 123; monopoly, 144; restrictions of, 150; trade, 131, 143

Harfleur, 131

Harvesting, 45

Hearth tax, 74–75

Hemp, 71

Henry I (1100–1135), 8

Henry II (1154–89), 8

Henry IV (1399–1413), 138

Henry the Navigator, 67, 161

Herding, 32, 39–41, 52, 62

Herring, 123

Hides, 41–42, 135

Hijaz, 155

Höchstetter, 122

Holland, 100–102, 148

Honey, 125

Hundred Years' War, 10, 21, 50–51, 53, 56, 58, 64, 70, 85, 102, 133–34, 147, 157

Hungary: 101; silver, 114

Humanism, 165–67

Hus, John, and mines, 114

Iberian Peninsula: 15, 65, 156, 161; monetary restrictions, 150; rainfall, 16; specie export, 146; trade, 117

India, 155, 163

Individual: 2, 4, 13, 164–65; and economic organization, 3; and guilds, 108; and law, 6; ordinary, 170; and papacy, 6; soul, 2; worker, 168

Industry: 73–115; rural, 46

Inferno, 10

Inheritance effect of plague, 82–83, 85, 87–89, 99, 103, 105, 111, 135

Instruments, commercial, 117; *see also* Credit; Exchange

Interest, 120

Iron, 124

Irrigation, 65, 71

Issoudun, guilds, 108

Italy: 63–70, 72, 122, 134, 138, 150, 153, 157–60, 162; agriculture, 135; bankers, 151; Black Sea, 117; cloth, 64; coin export, 143; credit, 121; English money, 142; fashion, 135; investment, 88; jewelry, 128; naval power, 147; plague, 27; sea route, 133; topography, 14; towns, 73; trade 125, 128; wool, 99

Ivory, 126, 128, 142, 163

Jacquerie, 56

Japan, 159

Jean le Bon (1350–64), 54, 85

Jerusalem, 169

Jewels, 91, 126, 128, 142

Jews, 121, 132

Joan of Arc, 122

John I (1199–1216), 7

John I (Portugal), 161

Juiverie, Rue de la, 78

Khan, Great, 159

Labor: costs, 34, 55, 57; laws, 50; mobility restricted, 11, 46; and plague, 10; services, 10, 33, 43, 60
Laborers, Statute of, 45
La Rochelle: guilds, 108; wine, 123
Law: abstract, 166; canon, 119, 167; customary, 165; divine, 2, 4, 6, 13, 108, 167; and guilds, 108; King subject to, 8; natural, 6, 108; and revolt, 107; Roman, 6, 165–66; sumptuary, 136, 168
Leather making, 84
Legacies to Church, 103, 138, 144
Legislation: agricultural, 69; bullion, 89; food, 77–78; labor, 30, 45, 50, 51, 56, 61, 168–69; market, 99; migration, 30; monetary, 140–41, 168; origins, 165; sumptuary, 149, 156–57; town, 96, 167
Legumes, 38
Leicester Abbey, 38
Lerida, pop., 76
Levant, 116, 126, 153, 155–56
Leyden, 101
Libelle of Englyshe Polycye, 142
Liberties, 107, 166
Lincoln, 97
Lincolnshire, 34
Linen, 57
Lisbon, 133
Livestock, 48, 52
Livonia, fur, 124
Loans: 119, 120; forced, 154; taxes, 56; wool, 93
Loire, 18
Lombard: 67, 70, 121, 154; cloth, 127; goods seized, 132; letters of, 142
London: 15, 41, 50, 97, 121, 133; famine, 80; markets, 78; Medici, 152; monetary conference, 145; pop., 73–74; silk, 103; spices, 127; testaments, 85, 87, 138
Longbow, 1, 124, 147
Looms, 98
Louis XI: 107; guilds, 108; Lyons, 133; regulation, 11; silk, 150
Louis XIV, 4
Louis of Nevers, 98

Louvre, 135
Low Countries: 15, 63, 92, 124; cloth, 137; imports, 123
Lübeck, 144
Lucca, silk, 103, 126–27
Lunebourg, Diet of (1412), 143
Luzzatto, Gino, 99
Luxury: 86, 91–92, 102, 104, 112, 126, 135–37, 142–44, 148–49, 153, 155–57; consumption, 89; crops, 65; production, 71; spices, 127; trade, 110, 117, 154
Lyons: fairs, 133; Medici, 152

Machiavelli, 165
Madeiras, 67, 159, 161
Magdeburg, pop., 81
Magna Carta: mercenaries, 8; property, 7
Malaria, 66, 87
Malthus, 23
Maremma, 23
Marseille: cloth, 94; guilds, 108; trade, 129–30
Marsilius of Padua, 6, 167
Martin V, Pope, 145
Meat, 32, 38, 40, 86
Medici: 104, 152; bank, 121, 151, 158; silk, 105; smuggling, 142; Venice, 153
Mediterranean: 15, 110, 116, 125, 144, 147, 150, 154, 157–60, 162; charts, 133; commerce, 118, 127; credit, 119–20; Turks, 134
Mercantilism, 11
Mercenaries, 8–9
Merchants: 111–12, 116; credit, 118, 120; foreign, 168; Genoese, 156; guilds, 110; Hanseatic, 133, 143; individual, 161; Italian, 121, 123, 149; loans, 119; Lübeck, 144; views, 141
Merino sheep, 62, 64, 99, 126
Mesta, 62–64
Metallurgy, 84
Metals: 126; monetary, 114; precious, 102, 113, 122, 137–38, 142, 144, 147–48, 150; trade, 125
Migration, 27, 30, 46, 57, 66, 79, 90

Milan: 71, 144, 153; arms, 70, 128, 156; Medici, 152; money exports, 147; pop., 73; silk, 103, 127; trade, 125
Military: efficiency, 8–9; strategy, 1; technology, 9, 12
Milk, 59
Ming Dynasty, 104, 134
Mining, 111–15, 150
Mint, Venetian, 154
Mocenigo, Doge Tomaso, 154–55
Modena, pop., 76
Money: 48, 55, 60; bimetallic, 122; coinage, 89; export, 5, 12, 149–50, 168; loans, 121; movements, 123; scarcity, 101, 145; stability, 119; taxes, 56, 75
Mongol, 104
Montpellier: guilds, 108; pop., 76
Moors, 65
More, Sir Thomas, 34
Mulberry trees, 71

Naples: Medici, 152; pop., 73
Narbonne, pop., 76
Naval expense, 4
Near East, 117
Netherlands, 18, 123
Newgate, 78
New World, 162
Nogaret, 5
Norfolk, rents, 30
Norias, irrigation, 65
Normandy, guilds, 108
North Africa: trade, 125; wool, 126
North Sea, 123
Norway, 58–59
Novgorod, 125
Nuremberg: 143–44; clothiers, 101; trade, 125
Nutrition, 81

Oak, ships, 123
Oats, 38–39
Oil, olive, 67
Oranges, 68
Orchards, and war, 52
Ordinance of 1349, 45
Oxford, 34, 97

Paris: 51, 73, 85; guilds, 108; markets, 78; Parlement of, 146
Partnership, 118, 121
Pazzi, 151
Peas, 38–39
Peasants: 45–48, 56, 60–61, 72, 79; in cities, 70; credit, 69; diet, 49; earnings, 49; southern Italy, 66
Pepper, 127, 163
Percy Estates, revenues, 47
Perpiñan, pop., 76
Peruzzi, 121, 151–52, 158
Pestilence, 91, 145; *see also* Plague
Peter's Pence, 145
Philip Augustus (1180–1223), 117
Philip IV (1285–1314), 1; confiscates Gascony, 4; Dante, 10; mercenaries, 9; price control, 78; Order of the Temple, 121; taxation, 5, 132
Philip VI (1328–50), 12
Philip the Good, 101
Phocaea, 126
Pigs, 57
Pisa, Medici, 152
Pistoia, 30–31
Plague: 2, 27, 34, 36–38, 45–46, 48–49, 55, 66, 70, 80–81, 84–87, 91, 103, 105, 137, 145, 149, 155, 159, 162, 168; and balance of payments, 12; England, 29; guilds, 111; labor, 10; luxury, 136; markets, 95; merry life, 88; mining, 114; prosperity, 112; skill, 83; trade, 131, 134–35; urban economy, 11
Plowing, 20, 45
Poitiers: Battle of (1356): 9, 52; guilds, 108
Poland, 60, 123–24
Poles, 160
Political theory, 1–2, 5–6, 165, 167
Polo, Marco, 104, 159
Ponthieu, coin export, 150
Population: 22, 29, 32, 42, 58, 61–62, 70–71, 74, 90, 98, 111–12, 148, 157, 159, 162, 167, 169; Catalonia, 28; and cloth, 102; density, 92; eastern Europe, 101; England, 19, 28; Europe, 20; food, 25; Germany, 57; growth, 77, 91, 150; labor, 82; and legacies, 88; and markets, 93, 97; mining,

Population (*cont.*)
114; Pistoia, 31; Poland, 60; Russia, 60; and taxes, 75; trade, 131; urban, 73, 76, 81; and wool, 96
Portugal, 16, 160–63
Postan, M., 25
Poultry, 38
Po Valley, 14, 16, 21, 70, 79
Pragmatic Sanction (1438), 146
Prester John, 160
Prices: agricultural, 10, 50, 54, 90, 135; armor, 128; beer, 35; bread, 36, 39, 84; butter, 40, citrus, 68; control, 78; fish, 60; food, 103, 157; fur, 138; grain, 25–26, 29, 34, 36, 53, 57–59, 62–63, 66, 70, 78, 81, 86, 89, 90, 93; hides, 42, 84; indices, 89; industrial, 90; labor, 10, 29–30, 32–34, 44–45, 93; manufactures, 89–90, 135; meat, 40–41; pepper, 163; pork, 58; produce, 145; raised by Turks, 157; regulated, 109; silk, 104, 126; sugar, 162; wine, 55, 135; wool, 35, 63, 96
Productivity, 82, 86, 91
Prohibition on imports, 142
Property: 164, 170; Aquinas on, 3; justified, 2; and law, 6; and *Magna Carta*, 7
Protectionism, 99, 106–7
Provins, 120
Provisionment, 77, 79, 80–81
Prussia, 61
Puigcerda, pop., 76
Purveyance, 50
Pyrenees, 15

Queenhithe, 78

Ragusa, 79
Rainfall, 15, 18
Ramsey Abbey, 36, 38–39
Rebellion, 168
Reformation, 165
Regrating, 77
Regulation: 105; cloth, 98; economic, 170; food, 78–79; guilds, 85; municipal, 106; trade, 106
Reincke, 81
Renaissance, 164–67
Rent: 30, 43–44, 47, 53–54, 72, 81, 90;

Rent (*cont.*)
church, 69, 169; inflation and, 10; monetary, 10; Norway, 59
Restrictionism: 99, 105–6, 111–12, 167; guild, 109, 168; import, 142; Italians, 143, 150; labor, 168; Peter's Pence, 145
Revenues: Durham, 47; land, 49
Revolt: agrarian, 56; urban, 106–7
Rice, 68
Richard II (1377–99), 11, 50, 135
Riga, 138
Rioting, urban, 107
Robbins, H., 26
Roman: agriculture, 65; Empire and guilds, 109; mining, 113
Rome: 15, 67, 144–46, 169; bankers, 151; Medici, 152–53
de Roover, R., 104, 152
Rotterdam, cloth, 101
Rouen, 85, 108
Routiers, 53
Royal: authority, 11; regulation, 7, 11–12
Rucellai, 151
Russell, J. C., 19
Russia: 25, 60; fur, 124; soil, 16; trade, 117
Rye, 59

Sacraments, 2
St. Germain-des-Prés, 30
Salt, 84, 123, 133
Savoy, 148
Saxony, 114
Scandinavia: 16, 59; beer, 58; forest, 124; fur, 124; towns, 74
Schism, 6, 145–46, 166
Scholasticism, 2
Scotland, 4, 16
Seed/Yield ratio, 24–25, 37, 39
Senegal, 160, 162
Sens, 108
Serbia, 114
Serfdom, second, 61
Sheep: 34, 63–64, 96, 126; pasture, 55; raising, 62, 71
Sherborne, 36
Shipping, 70, 124, 132–33, 156, 158

Ships: 59, 66, 123, 125, 133–34, 156, 158–59; builders, 123, 155

Shoemakers, 83, 85

Sicily, 23, 66, 70, 125

Siena, pop., 75–76

Sigismund, Emperor (1410–37), 114

Silk: 65, 92, 102, 104–5, 111–12, 126–28, 135–38, 142, 144, 150, 155–56; Florentine, 103

Silver: 113, 125; coin, 120, 122, 137, 154; exports, 138, 150; mining, 114

Skill, 85

Slaves, 85, 162–64

Sluys, Battle of (1340), 58

Soil: 17, 162; erosion, 24; fertility, 45; types, 16

Southampton, 133

Spain: 15–16, 61–65, 67; forests, 16; Genoa and, 158; guilds, 110; plague, 27; silk, 104; specie exports, 147; topography, 14; wool, 99, 126

Spice Islands, 163

Spices, 86, 127, 136, 156

Spinners, 82

Stock-raising, 38, 41–42, 58

Strategy, military, 51

Strozzi, 151

Subinfeudation, 8

Sugar, 65–68, 125, 162

Sumptuary laws: 136, 149, 157, 168; Venice, 156

Sussex, 47

Sweden, 15

Swineherding, 57

Switzerland, 14

Syria, 155

Taille, 54

Tannenberg, Battle of (1410), 100–101

Tanning, 84, 108

Tariffs, 157

Tarragona, pop., 76

Taxation: 50, 56, 90, 154, 170; agriculture, 50, 90, 135; church, 4–5; death, 41; direct, 168; hearth, 107; Mesta, 62; nobles impose, 6; ransom and, 54; resisted, 6, 54, 56, 107; rolls, 74; sales, 132; towns, 12, 69, 72–73, 75

Technology: agriculture, 18, 20–21, 25, 52, 65–66; desire for, 159; industry, 83; military, 51, 124, 168; mining, 112–14, 150; salt, 84; shipping, 132–33, 158, 160; towns, 74; transportation, 124

Temple, Order of the, 121

Teutonic Knights, 100

Textiles: 63, 88, 96–97, 127; Florence firms, 99

Three-field system, 17–18, 20–21, 24, 59, 61

Threshing, 45

Thuringia, 57

Timber, 125–26, 137, 153, 157

Titow, J., 25

Topography, 14–15

Toulouse: 55, 78; pop., 76

Tours, 108

Towns: 53–54, 57, 70, 73–115; food for, 23; Hanse, 59, 131, 138, 143–44; invest in land, 72; legislation, 167; luxury, 135; pop., 21–22; regulation, 7, 12; and strength of king, 8

Trade: 74, 82; fur, 101; grain, 68, 79; international, 60, 112, 114–63; interregional, 127; patterns, 110–11; silk, 104; statistics, 129–31; terms of, 138; volume, 149

Trèves, 143

Turkestan, silk, 126

Turks: 104, 125, 158; and Atlantic, 160; Constantinople, 157; expand, 153; trade, 134

Tuscany, 23

Unam Sanctam, 5

Urals, 15

Urine, 97

Valencia, pop., 76

Velocity of circulation, 122, 148

Velvet, 102, 127, 137

Venice: 71, 79, 144, 155–58, 160; food, 23; luxury, 70; Medici, 152–53; pop., 73, 76; silk, 103, 127; taxes, 154; trade, 125

Verde, Cape, 161

Vestments, 103, 144

Veulerent, 55, 68
Villani, Matteo, 87
Vineyards, 52, 55, 133–34
Vivaldi brothers, 159

Wales, 4
Wars of the Roses, 11
Water power, 84, 96
Wax, 138, 143–44
Weavers: 82, 99; guilds, 110
Welser, 122
West Country, 96
Wheat: 37, 39, 53, 59, 104; German, 58; Sicilian, 162
White, Lynn, 17
Wilburton, 47
William I, the Conqueror (1066–87), 7
Winchester: 39, 42; Bishop of, 25, 37
Wine: 32, 55, 57–58, 68, 71, 86, 121,

Wine (*cont.*)
123, 135; Madeira, 67; prices, 134; trade, 133
Wistow, 25
Woad, 67, 71
Wool: 34–35, 63, 92–93, 96, 98–99, 105, 121, 124, 126, 135, 137; compared to silk, 105; exports, 12, 63–64; woolsacks, 93
Woolen, 83, 98, 112, 127, 137

Yemen, 155
Yields, agricultural, 24
York, 97
Yorkshire, 34, 96
Ypres: 63–64, 92, 97; cloth, 94–95, 98; famine, 26, 80

Zurich, pop., 76
Zwin, 143